Praise for *Stolen Jesus*

When the grace of God collides with our candid admission of failure, the result is often laughter and joy. *Stolen Jesus* does not shy away from the hurts inflicted by messed-up religion, yet this is the funniest Christian book I have read. Thank God for honest authors like Jami Amerine who are brave enough to write about life as it is.

Paul Ellis, author of *Stuff Jesus Never Said*

Stolen Jesus will steal your heart and compel you to keep turning the pages. If you feel as though you are on shaky ground in your walk with Jesus, this book will leave you standing on solid ground.

Anna LeBaron, author of *The Polygamist's Daughter*

As mere mortals, we tend to create different versions of Jesus from our own experiences. Jami's fearless and funny categorization of her collection of different Jesuses is something to experience. Not only will you want to pay real money just to be in the backseat of her car during her next Starbucks run (because you will…), but this book will make you want to go deeper—truly examining your own Jesus collection and paring it down to one, true, Savior.

Kathi Lipp, author of *The Husband Project, Clutter Free,* and *Overwhelmed*

Jami Amerine announces, "I broke up with Jesus!" She does a good job of saying the things we all feel. Of searching for what we all want to find. And of refusing to settle for easy answers. I started reading her journey and ended up journeying right along with her. Thank you, Jami, for your humorously serious quest to find the Real Jesus.

Kay Marshall Strom, 21st century abolitionist

Jami's search for Jesus is authentic, vulnerable, and heart touching. She rips off clean and tidy façades, fights legalism, and hits back against backbreaking shame. Expect to go through these pages laughing, arriving at the last page loved and liberated.

K

Thank God that Jesus is not who I made Hi
coaster deity that was hormonal and enjo
line. *Stolen Jesus* is delightful freedom to al

D1407972

by fakes, phonies, or counterfeits of the True Savior. Come away from the crazy by entering Jami's crazy as you snort with laughter, cry with relief, and uncover Real Jesus in all His glory.

Katie Reid, *author of Made Like Martha*

It's beautiful. It's authentic. It's delightful. It's honest. I chuckled and gasped and reflected and got covered in goose bumps. Every few pages, I found myself taking a break and pacing the floor to give my head a moment to catch up with what was happening in my heart. This book is a captivating story of a grace encounter with the Real Jesus. It left me praising Him. Pondering Him. Conscious of His presence. Aware of His love. Knowing Him more. Loving Him more…without even trying.

Tricia Gunn, author of *Unveiling Jesus*

In this raw, hilarious, high-energy narrative, Jami Amerine describes the various Jesus aberrations that she has encountered in the American body of believers. These false Christs drive her to interminable God-pleasing works, requiring rigid perfection but instead generating shame, fear, and guilt. This was the perfect condition for Jami to finally discover the Real Jesus, who saves by grace.

Dr. Lynn Wilder, Ex-Mormon Christians United for Jesus

Jami Amerine will take you by surprise. She'll say what no one else is willing to say, reveal what no one else is willing to reveal, and do it in a manner that is self-deprecating, completely authentic, and emotionally real. Prepare yourself for an adventure.

Jan Greenwood, author of *Women at War*

I love a writer who tells the raw truth, shows her flaws and foibles, and keeps you smiling and hanging on every word! *Stolen Jesus* will have you laughing and nodding your head in agreement one minute and wiping away tears the next. Searching is good, questioning is good, but know that there *are* answers and Jami's book will help you find them. You'll come away wanting to know the Real Jesus.

Kate Battistelli, author of *Growing Great Kids*

Jami Amerine takes the reader on a tender, riveting, multifaceted journey in *Stolen Jesus*. The Jesus she discovers in the new covenant is like a cool glass of water after spending years in a relentless fiery furnace. There nothing mundane about this author and absolutely nothing boring in the poignant words of *Stolen Jesus*.

Tracy Levinson, author of *Unashamed*

STOLEN JESUS

JAMI AMERINE

HARVEST HOUSE PUBLISHERS
EUGENE, OREGON

Interior design by Janelle Coury

Cover design by Bryce Williamson

Cover Image © grinvalds, germi_p / iStock

Published in association with Kirkland Media Management, LLC. P.O. Box 1539, Liberty, Texas 77575

STOLEN JESUS

Published by Harvest House Publishers
Eugene, Oregon 97402
www.harvesthousepublishers.com

ISBN 978-0-7369-7063-1 (pbk.)
ISBN 978-0-7369-7064-8 (eBook)

Library of Congress Cataloging-in-Publication Data
Names: Amerine, Jami, author.
Title: Stolen Jesus / Jami Amerine.
Description: Eugene, Oregon : Harvest House Publishers, 2017. | Includes bibliographical references.
Identifiers: LCCN 2017011314 (print) | LCCN 2017030763 (ebook) | ISBN 9780736970648 (ebook) | ISBN 9780736970631 (pbk.)
Subjects: LCSH: Jesus Christ—Person and offices. | Amerine, Jami. | Christian biography.
Classification: LCC BT203 (ebook) | LCC BT203 .A528 2017 (print) | DDC 232—dc23
LC record available at https://lccn.loc.gov/2017011314

Printed in the United States of America

17 18 19 20 21 22 23 24 25 / BP-JC / 10 9 8 7 6 5 4 3 2 1

For Steve Murray—
Thanks for asking.

Contents

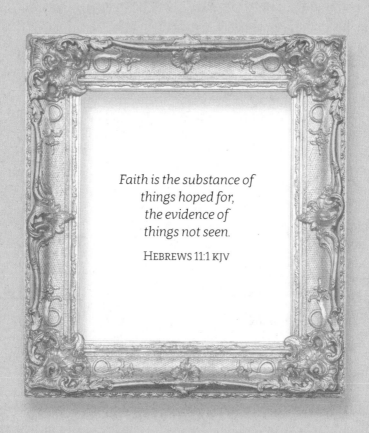

*Faith is the substance of
things hoped for,
the evidence of
things not seen.*

Hebrews 11:1 KJV

Foreword

As I set this book down (after reading through it in a single day), I realize what a gift I am holding. I've cried, laughed, smiled, and sighed with Jami through these pages. The REAL Jesus, the Jesus I want my children to grow up with, is right here. He is good. He is grace. He is everything.

I found Jami's blog years ago and felt an immediate connection. I laughed as I read that first blog post. I finished reading and immediately sent the link to at least seven of my friends. *Could this woman possibly be any more my kind of person?* Through the real moments we have all had as parents, Jami shares her heart and her Jesus with everyone she meets and keeps you laughing through it all.

This book is for the lifelong Christian who needs a little reminder of how real Jesus is in their everyday circumstances—but it isn't just for them. This book is also for the brand-new believer who still sees the world through shiny, rose-colored glasses. And this book is for everyone who "broke up with Jesus" years ago because they were looking at people and circumstances and not at Christ Himself.

If you've spent your life searching for Jesus in people and places and things, *Stolen Jesus* was written especially for you. Jami's journey is one we've all taken in our own ways. From church camp to college, from that first sweet child's prayer to the angry prayer we've cried in the midst of heartache, Jesus has been there for us every step along the way.

I share Jami's blog with as many people as I possibly can, and today I am thrilled to be able to share her book as well. It is an honor to be writing this foreword, and my prayer is that this book will touch your life as deeply as it has touched mine.

—Mary Younkin
author of *The Weeknight Dinner Cookbook*

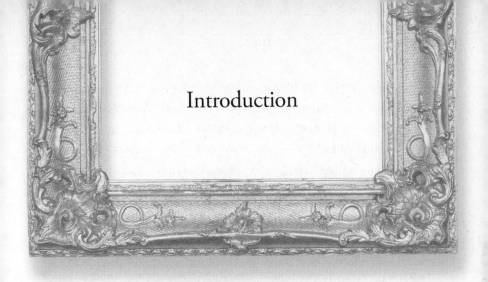

Introduction

You will know the truth, and
the truth will set you free.

JOHN 8:32 ESV

I broke up with Jesus."

I said it flippantly, perhaps for shock value, but it was true. Jesus and I weren't on speaking terms. Sitting at a table at a Christian writer's conference, I now had the full attention of my newfound friends. The jaded trio listened as I lamented my disdain for the letdowns and the broken promises—a litany of complaints that had led me to this place of defeat.

Worship music blared, and at the next table, rejected would-be authors sobbed into their chips and salsa. The three wordsmiths nodded and listened to me gripe. One of them was a magazine editor up to her neck in the "hypocrisy of the Christian elite." The next had battled drug addiction, rape, and mental terror and lived to write about it—eloquently. And the third was a wise, speak-your-mind-and-stop-making-excuses former missionary who asked hard questions and gave hard answers.

I ranted, "I write this stuff, but there's no solution. The feel-good, fix-yourself-or-else Jesus is a crutch. I am in bondage to donuts. I give and give, and it never gets any better. I follow the rules until I can't anymore, and I can't keep up my end of the bargain. I thought my brand was going to be Snarky Jesus Girl, but honestly, I am more into Pilates. So, I broke up with Jesus."

Ex-missionary gave a snort, demanding my attention.

"What?" I asked.

She leaned toward me. "Jami, it's easy to break up with Americanized Jesus. It's impossible to break up with the Real Jesus."

Real Jesus?

Wasn't that who I was worshipping? Wasn't that who I lived for? What was she even talking about? For the better part of forty years, Jesus was all I had been devoted to. My driving goal had been to serve and please the Son of God.

Maybe I'd been worshipping the wrong god all along.

Unbeknownst to me at the time, the conversation was the beginning step out of the prison cell and into the banquet hall. That ex-missionary's statement would change everything. That moment would set me on a road of discovery that would finally uncover all I had missed in my quest to know Jesus.

This book is an account of the unraveling of all the ways I embraced characteristics that robbed me of the actual character of the risen Lord and the message of the cross. In these pages I invite you to travel with me through the insanity that is my life and the unique way I have intermingled with the Jesuses created by my mind and experiences. I am not here to talk you into or out of any religion or belief. I am here to tell you a story, an ongoing story of discovery. You will journey with me and Stolen Jesus, Mormon Jesus, Catholic Jesus, Americanized Jesus, Fifth-Grade Jesus, and a wealth of other characters that all paved the way to the Real Jesus. All leading to the magnificent capstone: He is real.

However, knowing Him doesn't involve a finish line. This relationship is a lifelong quest, a quest that can be beautifully decorated with the essence of our creation—to be with Him for eternity.

Before you read any further, know this: There is only one Jesus. He is consistent and pure. When the Real Jesus shows up, He is unmistakable. This book is not permission for you to make Him into who you want Him to be. This book is a peek at what it looks like to let Him just be. Be still, let go, laugh, cry...grieve and rejoice.

Let's journey back to a time when Jesus was becoming more than just a story to you, to a place of wonder, the place where you first met Him. If you have never met Him, I am honored to introduce you to Him. But first, lay down every portrayal of Him that has hurt you, lied to you, misled you, or betrayed you, and let's separate those counterfeit Christs from the One who literally died for you.

I can tell you a million stories about my dad. He is a grand adventurer, geologist, hunter, and seeker of truth. He loves my mom and playing with his grandkids. But unless you meet him for yourself, unless you spend forty-five years as his daughter, you can't understand what my dad and I share.

I propose that is the truth of Jesus as well. It will take us a lifetime of knowing Him and an eternity of worshipping to understand the depths of the Messiah. Maybe for you, like me, Jesus has taken on a personality formulated by internal and external factors, heavily influenced by your wiring, upbringing, and chance encounters with well-meaning humans who are struggling just like you...and occasionally robbing you of Real Jesus in the process.

Envision, for just a moment, if all the damage to His true character could be restored. Imagine yourself reclaiming that which He meant for your ultimate joy—joy He intended for you to tap into so you could live in freedom. Fancy what He would look like if you could separate Him from the Christians, non-Christians, and everyday Joes who have let you down, broken your heart, misled you, and wrecked you and your spirit.

In the end, the journey is yours. Open your mind; loosen the guard on your heart. Chances are, there is at least one characteristic you have attached to the risen Lord that has nothing to do with who He is and why He died for you. Too often, I know, I try to morph the Great I AM into someone with whom I can drink lattes before Pilates.

I will begin with a list of my shortcomings so that you will not read this book as if it were a how-to or a book of advice. These pages don't contain secret, time-saving tidbits to make your life easier. I wish I could say this book holds the recipe by which I was made entirely perfect. That in these pages lies the secret of how I manage to be up by four thirty in the morning, donning a ruffled linen apron around my sixteen-inch waist. I wish I could tell you that you could drop by my house and find me baking gluten-free muffins and packing nutritious, delicious, Pinterest-approved lunches while bluebirds chirp from their perch on my kitchen windowsill. That I accomplish this all in an A-line polka-dot dress, pantyhose, and four-inch red stilettos, my hair in a fancy up-do, my makeup and lipstick impeccable. And that, of course, my children are always dressed, pressed, and ready to impress.

Alas, this is not the case. No, in the pages of this book lies the truth of what it looks like to love Jesus and live in reality. The reality that Satan uses to make me feel less, to silence me so as not to shout "Glory!" to the blameless Father I have in heaven. Furthermore, the reality that I have allowed to shape Jesus into a one-dimensional Bible story with no joy but boundless criticisms.

I don't want to lose you down that chasm of comparison where you begin to think, *Well, isn't she sweet, wise, and superb! Here's yet another book by a superspiritual wonder woman.* Let me assure you, I am a disaster. I have some inadequate parenting stories (not bad as in Child Welfare bad, but certainly not Mom of the Year stories), some of which I will share with you in the coming pages.

There are crayon drawings on my walls. There are currently four basketfuls of laundry on the dining room table and a mountain of dirty dishes in the sink. Some days I make beautiful meals, and lots of other days we get takeout. Sometimes it's McDonald's.

I can't be your hero or teacher—no one would want a hero who was such a hot mess. On the bright side, at least you won't be distracted from the goal of coming face-to-face with Jesus Christ.

I pray this book will be a testimony to His pure grace in the crazy. And although I am no theologian, this much I will stand by, and this much I hold dear: He created you for fellowship with Him. He is a friend of sinners. The work was accomplished on the cross. You are never so far outside His reach that He will not answer when you call. He will meet you on the side of the road with a blown-out tire and hungry, cranky kids, and He is with you when you are flat on your back in the laundry room, begging for mercy. You cannot shock, irritate, or exasperate Him because He loves you—unto His death.

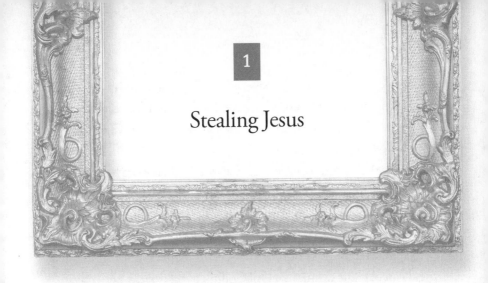

1

Stealing Jesus

Thus says the LORD who made the earth,
the LORD who formed it to establish it—
the LORD is his name: Call to me and I will
answer you, and will tell you great and
hidden things that you have not known.

JEREMIAH 33:2-3 ESV

I am a walking contradiction. Let's establish this from the start.

I am a lover of Jesus and abundant joy. I am a wife and mother of six, maybe seven or eight. A homeschooler and PTA mom. An aerobics instructor and binge eater. A marathon runner this week; a champion puff-pastry artist the next. I have a type A personality with type C tendencies. I'm a vegan on Monday, and an "I'll take my steak rare!" lunatic by Friday. I am a cattle ranch owner who loves city living. I'm a blacklisted Mormon and a displaced Catholic attending an instrumental Church of Christ. (That means lots of toe tapping and banjo strumming.)

I worship at the feet of a genie-in-a-bottle Jesus when the line at Starbucks gets too long and I am going to be late to Pilates. And

I bawl like a baby when we have to turn away a foster placement, unable to help a child in need. I have a degree in home economics, but I can't thread a needle. I can make yeast rolls that would drive you to weep. I am allergic to wheat.

I want the warm, cozy feelings I experience in my prayer chair to last forever, but I am tightly wound. I am a worrier. And I am terrified of many things—vomit, flying, roller coasters, crunchy bugs, and egg salad primarily.

My mortal claim to fame is that even though I've had no training, I can play the drums like Phil Collins, and I can rap perfectly in sync to the Beastie Boys, *all of their songs*. And I can do that without missing a lick after a worship singalong with Francesca Battistelli. The weight of this paradox is not lost on me.

I seem to fail at many things. And when I don't fail, I get so bolstered with pride, it is sinful. My entire existence is a study in contradictions.

And yet I tread on the sacred. My reality doesn't change who Jesus is. I propose we are so used to making Him fit our world and our brains that we have missed out on experiencing the richness of Him. Our society, busy minds, bad theology, and first-world living have robbed us of a priceless commodity. And what's been taken from us? Jesus. The *real* Jesus.

So here I am. An almost high school dropout with a master's degree. A dyslexic author. A foot racer with bad knees and broken arches. I am filling out college scholarship applications for two children and preschool submissions for another while bouncing a newborn in a sling (and did I mention I don't have a uterus?). I am certified to teach eleven different aerobics classes, but I need to lose sixty pounds. I crave honesty and a rawness I don't always find in the church pew, yet I try to never miss a Sunday. And I believe in being nice, and obeying the law—and still, I stole Jesus.

My first image of Jesus came from the Mormon church. *Head of Christ*, the famous painting by Walter Sallman, hung in every ward (the neighborhood church) and also in the Mormon temple. This is still the image I see whenever I hear the name of Jesus. Over the years, long after I left the Mormon church, I would occasionally see this familiar painting of what I thought of as "Mormon Jesus," and I felt as if I were seeing an old friend.

Then, in 2005, I began to teach aerobics classes at a local YMCA. I was delighted the first time I walked into the lobby and was greeted by the painting. One afternoon, after I taught a cycling class, I was clocking out when I noticed that the portrait of Jesus was gone. It had been replaced with a dry-erase board.

Confused—because the joint is a Christian organization and the sweet face of our Christ was constantly in view—I asked the receptionist, "Where's Jesus?"

"Oh! He's behind the filing cabinet." She pointed toward the back of the office. "Management thinks He's too old-fashioned."

So, sneaking Him out unseen, I took Stolen Jesus home with me.

Now He hangs over the mantel, a fugitive from the YMCA, and we are proud to have Him there. On many occasions, I have sat in our living room and talked to Stolen Jesus, the Jesus I made my own when He was rejected. With His rock-star mullet, dreamy blue eyes, and olive complexion, He is calm and constant. He never seems bothered or troubled.

His familiar presence changes things. Once my husband and I got into an argument in the living room, and we quickly remembered Stolen Jesus was watching. I said, "We really shouldn't yell in front of Stolen Jesus..." So, we moved to the kitchen and forgot what we were arguing about. Sometimes we catch ourselves: "Don't say that in front of Stolen Jesus!" Or I'll chirp to one of our toddlers, Sam and Charlie, whom we lovingly call the Vandals, "Really? You're naked in front of Stolen Jesus?" And I know Jesus is much more than a moral compass, much more than a painting. But to have Him in our living room is a reminder of who we should be...who I wish I was.

As much as I have grown to know and love that image, it wasn't until we began our journey in foster care that I realized I didn't know Jesus as well as I thought I did. It occurred to me that I had given Him characteristics based on human interactions. I had waited for others to explain Him to me. Worse still, I had allowed Him to be stolen *from me.* And it was at the end of one terrible day that I came to the realization I needed to get to know Him on my own.

The morning started out poorly. My husband, Justin, and I don't argue a lot, but on this certain morning we'd gotten into a full-blown battle about disciplining one of the kids. Justin had taken away our middle son Luke's phone. While I was in agreement about the need for training, the loss of that particular phone really punished *me.* This child would almost certainly nag me to death until his phone was returned to him. Moreover, I would be unable to reach him on a day he had two appointments. Without his phone, I would have to unload babies from their car seats and venture up several flights of stairs in two different locations to retrieve him. Of course, I could make other provisions for him, but at the moment the phone was confiscated, I was dismayed.

Sophie, who was twelve at the time, was cranky over some missing papers, and when Sophie gets cranky, *just stand back*. (I cannot imagine where she gets the drama gene.) John and his brother Luke, both in their early teens, were bickering in the kitchen over the last piece of bacon, and both Sam, a toddler, and our foster son had been up and down several times during the night. (We hadn't adopted Charlie yet, but if he'd been in the picture, he would have been a mess too.) As I was getting everyone into the car, Justin barked, "Are you taking the baby to the doctor so we can get some sleep?"

I yawned back at him and said, "No. I don't have time today, and I think he's just teething."

Justin barked, "Well, *perfect*! I forgot he has to get teeth!"

I glared at him while he stormed past me, slamming the door. I sighed heavily. I was forty-three years old, with a borrowed newborn, and honestly, teething had slipped my mind too...that and potty training. But I wasn't about to let Justin know that.

I drove the kids to school. I looked a fright. I hadn't gotten up before the children, and I was still wearing my pajamas. I hadn't put on a bra, and my dirty Ugg boots adorned my already tired feet. We pulled up to the school, and John asked, "Can you come inside to sign my permission slip?"

I am not a woman who can go without a bra, so I explained to my son that I would *not* be going into the office. This vexed John, apparently more than having his braless, pajama-clad mother inside his school, but he grouchily agreed to bring the permission slip out to me. The wait in the office for the slip caused him to be tardy, which did nothing to improve anyone's mood.

As I drove the babies home, I couldn't stop yawning, fantasizing about the huge cup of coffee I'd enjoy while the babies played and I dozed in my prayer chair with Stolen Jesus.

Coffee. Coffee. Coffee. And then...

And then I remembered: I hadn't gone to the store the day before. We were out of coffee.

We were out of coffee.

Trying not to cry, I hopped on the drive-thru loop for Starbucks. I pulled up in line behind forty cars. Thirty minutes later I ordered *two* venti coffees, which would enable me to guzzle coffee until noon. Mustering a smile, I advanced to the window to pay. To my horror, I realized I didn't have my wallet. And I started to cry.

The barista took pity on what was clearly a desperate situation and said, "Uh, it's okay, ma'am. This one's on the house!" Weeping with gratitude and humiliation, but with coffee in hand, I vowed that I'd be back that afternoon to pay for my order. I cried and drove, talking out loud to myself or Americanized Jesus about my first-world problems. As I turned onto my street, I noticed a blue car sitting in front of our house. *Who in the world is that?* I drove past the car to pull into the garage and realized it was the foster baby's caseworker from Child Welfare.

Surprise inspection.

"You have got to be *kidding* me!" I said out loud, this time directly to Jesus.

I closed the garage and got Sam and the baby out of their car seats. They were both still in their jammies, and both looked a little...*crusty.* But there was no time for a bra or a change of clothes; the caseworker was already ringing the doorbell.

I begrudgingly let her into the house, apologizing for being such a mess. I explained that we'd had a rough night and a harsh morning while she wrote something down on her yellow notepad. *Really?* I offered her a seat in the living room, casting a cold stare at Stolen Jesus and mouthing the words, "Dude, help!" I spread a blanket on the floor for the baby and sat next to him. Sam talked gibberish to the caseworker for a minute, and I told him to please go watch Elmo.

Notepad in hand, the caseworker started in on about a thousand questions to which I responded while playing with the baby. At about the moment I thought the whole experience could not get any worse, Sam came in carrying a glass jar of pickles from Costco, about the same size as Sam himself. He also held a fork, a knife, a spoon, and, because he is not an animal, a napkin. He came to a stop directly over the baby, whose cranium was in full jeopardy of being squashed by the fifteen-pound jar of pickles.

The caseworker leaped out of her chair and snatched up the blameless babe just as the huge jar slipped to the ground where baby's head had been. Without missing a lick, I joked, "Nice save!"

Innocently, Sam said, "Mommy, bweakfas?" The look on the caseworker's face shifted from horror to disbelief as I pried open the jar of pickles and began feeding them to Sam, picnic-style, on the floor in the formal living room. But her incredulity was wasted on me. Surely this could not have been the worst environment she would see that day?

Taking the baby back from the caseworker, I answered her questions about our evacuation plans in the event of fire, nuclear war, or civil unrest. (Yes, this is for real.) She collected her notepad and stood up, asking to see the baby's bed and our fire extinguishers. Carrying Baby, I led her back to our room to show her the baby's crib, which was when I spotted them:

Rolaids.

They were on Justin's nightstand; she saw them too. She gasped. I'm not even exaggerating: The woman *gasped*. "Oh dear!" she said. "I'm going to have to write you up for this infraction. When I get back to the office, I will notify my supervisor about the unsecured medications. We'll have to meet to discuss it with licensing."

Being written up for the near death-by-pickles, I would have understood, but *Rolaids*? That was my last straw for the day, and it was only nine o'clock, which is pretty early for the last straw.

Feeling both exasperated and feisty, I pounced. "I'm sure my husband just forgot to put them up, and this baby can't walk or crawl. And it's not narcotics—it's *antacid*."

She looked at me forebodingly, again scratching rebuke on her little yellow notepad. "Medications must be kept out of children's reach."

"Well, *technically*, since he cannot stand, it *is* out of his reach. And it's not like I was cooking meth!"

She considered me over her eyeglasses with condescension worthy of a librarian and continued writing.

Now I was the one who categorically needed some Rolaids, and I wanted my coffee. She finally left, and I knew I would be hearing from our caseworker any minute. I went to get the cold Starbucks from the car to nuke it. Plopping down in my prayer chair, I glared at Stolen Jesus, and I made this vow out loud: "If they pull our foster license and come get this baby, I am going to insist that they take the other children too—biological and adopted. And then I am getting back in bed and eating pickles and taking a nap."

Stolen Jesus didn't respond.

It wasn't long before the phone rang, and I had to explain the Rolaids thing. I ate pickles for lunch, and I didn't get a nap. I drudged through the rest of the day, loading up the babies and going to Starbucks to pay for the morning's coffee and to get a third venti to go. I ran my older son to his appointments without incident (despite his lack of a cell phone), grabbed some pizzas, and came home. By seven o'clock, the baby was in bed and so was I. Justin helped the others with homework, and at some point, we apologized to each other for our viciousness earlier in the day.

I felt like a loser. Later that night, unable to sleep, I got up and went to the kitchen. I grabbed some gluten-free, low-fat cookies and Reese's Peanut Butter Cups and headed to sit with Stolen Jesus.

I flipped open my Bible, but I didn't have the energy to search out any wisdom. I didn't have the strength to process anything. I certainly did not need a lesson in who begat whom. I just needed a single word to drown out the voices in my head as I listed my failures. A voice whispered, "He won't want to say anything to you after your awful day." And I agreed with that voice. And then my eyes landed on Matthew 5:3:

Blessed are the poor in spirit...

Chills ran up my spine. I looked up at Stolen Jesus. Everyone was asleep, and they'd seen me talk to Him on many occasions, but still, I whispered, "Is that for me?"

He didn't say anything.

"This was all a punishment, wasn't it?"

Blessed are the poor in spirit...

A lump rose in my throat. "I don't know You at all, do I? I have all of these voices in my head and characteristics I believe about You, but I don't know what's real. This ghastly condemnation I feel—is this from You? Mormon Jesus wouldn't want me to be obsessed with coffee...but You? Real Jesus? Do you rebuke people for drinking coffee? Are You mad about the Rolaids? Are You mad because I deliver kids to school in my pajamas? Are You just mad?"

Blessed are the poor in spirit...

I sat in silence, and in that moment I was relieved to admit I was falling behind. I *was* poor in spirit, but in my poverty He was calling me blessed.

It occurred to me that I'd believed in (and broken up with) a lot of Jesuses over the years, but never a Jesus who had called me blessed. I'd believed in a Mormon Jesus, and a High School Jesus, and Justin's Jesus...but never, I think, the Real Jesus. My heart was racing.

I was swamped with a deep need to start over, to go back to the first time I heard His name. I wanted to relearn Jesus at the lowest level of understanding. Baby talk. Small words. A simple unfolding. An evolution, getting to know Him based on what I was developmentally capable of understanding, not trying to grasp Him from a lofty theological view.

I confess that I'd often thought of spirituality as a race, with everyone else running faster and farther ahead of me. But I realized that I didn't need to rush to keep up. I could back up, slow down. Falling behind had to be better than faking belief. I wouldn't ask a new bride to speed ahead fifteen years. Take your time, burn dinner, fight over the checkbook, and watch movies holding hands.

Discover each other.

For years I had professed an adoration for Jesus Christ, but in my poor state, on that night, I knew it was more habit than a relationship, more culture than worship, more clan than companionship. And I was undone. I wanted to have a real come-to-Jesus. I wanted the experience to be as genuine as possible.

It was time for a whole new Jesus.

Real Jesus.

I promise I could feel Him in the room. My mind raced, and I begged the feeling to stay. I wished I could be someone else, someone who was able to be fully present all the time. Someone whose mind never wandered to grocery lists during the sermon, someone whose Bible reading was never interrupted with shrieks. I wanted the depth of that moment to last forever.

And then I heard our foster son begin to cry, and I cried too.

Blessed are the poor in spirit.

Fine, I decided. I couldn't exist in a hypnotic state of bliss and remain euphorically high on Jesus. I rushed to tend to the baby and rushed back to the chair and willed my mind back to the idyllic state I had experienced moments before the hollers.

I reached in my Bible study bag and pulled out a journal and pen, and I asked Real Jesus to show Himself to me. Words poured from the pen. Pleas emptied from my heart. Once the ball started rolling, there was no stopping the process. So much of what I embraced about Jesus had been formulated decades ago. Fear, shame, and legalism were definitely issues I needed to deal with. Out loud I said, "Search my heart. Help me start over! Help me escape the lies and the torture of letting You down every single day." My pen flew across the pages of the journal: "Bad things happen, good things happen, and He stays. *He is always here.*"

I wept and wrote. I confessed and begged. And sometime after three in the morning, I came to a place where I knew that as complex as I am, as diverse as my children are, so must be the One who fashioned us. He knows the flaws and inconsistencies that make me all Jami, all the time. From my lofty marathon goals to my adoration for Sunday naps and homemade pie, He is able to hold all my contradictions and weave them into one beautiful whole. The journey of discovery was just beginning.

I was startled from the reverie when Justin stumbled down the hall and said, "Geez, Jami, who in the world are you talking to in the middle of the night?"

Without hesitation, I blurted, "Just Jesus."

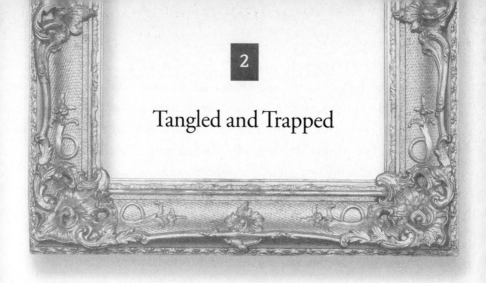

2

Tangled and Trapped

This is a people plundered and despoiled;
all of them are trapped in caves, or are
hidden away in prisons; they have become
a prey with none to deliver them, and a
spoil, with none to say, "Give them back!"

Isaiah 42:22 NASB

One day I got the older kids delivered to the school; I couldn't face Elmo or the laundry. I drove through Starbucks and then decided I would kill some time in my sanctuary: Target.

I remember it was windy. Here in West Texas just saying *windy* is an understatement, and the wind makes me crazy grumpy. I lose my focus, my head pounds, my nose stuffs up, and I am nasty to be around. I have zero tolerance for hot, sixty-mile-per-hour winds. None. And do not say, "You should move." I know; I totally should. However, I live here with my six or seven kids, and Justin's roots run deep, so I'm kind of stuck.

On this trip to Target, I had three small children with me: our three-year-old, Sam, our young foster son, and a foster toddler boy in our care for respite. (Respite foster care is when you take in a child to help another foster family that either needs a break or has something going on that prevents them from caring for the child for up to two weeks. This little guy was just with us for the day.) My goal was as follows: get in, get popcorn and Diet Coke, kill an hour until naptime, buy toilet paper, reinvent self with some Maybelline products, get out. Because it was windy, my "slump-attire" fully reflected my weather-related depression. My hair was in a tight topknot, and I wore yoga pants, an old T-shirt, and tennis shoes. I was altogether mopey.

Once inside, I realized there was only one cart available. I turned around and saw a pitiable Target employee chasing carts in the parking lot in the midst of a mini-tornado. Unquestionably, I wasn't going back out to try and rope one myself, even though that lone cart left in the store was from the early '90s. I loaded babies into the medieval contraption and gave it a shove, and it screeched forward. Metal on metal sparked across the linoleum. The babies shuddered.

I went to the concession counter to learn the popcorn popper was broken. The babies started screaming, "POPCORN! POPCORN! POPCORN!" Fearing a triple baby mutiny, I raced off to find some fruit chews. Turning the corner onto the fruit chew aisle, an older man saw my cart and remarked sagely, "That's a lot of babies. You know what causes that, right? You should hire a nanny."

Ah, yes. Three comments to delight the heart of a cranky, snarky mom. I bit back the following responses:

1. I know it's a lot of babies.

2. Yes, I know what causes this. Foster care and adoption. (But really? That is so icky to ask someone.)

3. I should hire a nanny! That is genius! Thank you, Einstein.

Instead of snark, I just gave him a shrug-laugh-sneer-smile combo while handing out a box of fruit chews to the babies. Without popcorn, I knew there would be no Maybelline makeover. The babies wouldn't stand for it.

I decided to cut my losses and just get toilet paper. What was left of the basket's wheels were grating to a halt. The only upshot of wheeling this disastrous cart was that I wouldn't need to go to the gym since I was getting my cardio and strength training all in one.

Using brute force on the cart, I made it to my destination, only to find a single package of prison-grade toilet paper left on the shelf. Spotting a young man in khakis and a red polo, I asked, "Where's all the toilet paper?"

He looked at me with annoyance and said, "I don't work here." Then he said, "You should get a different cart. That one is awful."

Oh joy. A new triumvirate of sass swarmed into my head.

1. Who wears a red polo and khakis to shop at Target?

2. Where the heck is all the toilet paper?

3. I should get a new basket! I wish I'd thought of that!

The only bright side? Diapers were buy two, get a $5 Target gift card. The economic rationale behind this ad campaign is basically nil, but it works on me like a kid in a candy store. The "on your next purchase" clause means I can come back and spend my winnings. The Target Jesus who blesses me with free monies is my hero. I believe he wants me to have all this made-in-China garbage because my material happiness makes him happy. Target Jesus, I praise you for the treasured red coupons I have been #blessed with.

Flush with the promise of multiple gift cards, I decided to buy a *lot* of diapers. Once I finally made it to the registers, the cashier made the mistake of saying, "You should get a different basket. That one is loud." I sent her a vicious glare.

After checking out, I left grumpy and unsatisfied—except for my coupons, of course. The rubber had now worn completely off the wheels of the cart. It was functioning like a train off its tracks. The friction caused repeated shocks, and the hair on two of the babies' heads was standing on end from the static. And the basket had another annoying feature—a broken piece of plastic that was jutting out, clipping me on the leg and literally adding injury to insult for this particular excursion.

We made it out to the van fighting both gale-force winds and the cart. I opened the back door and bent over to take a case of diapers out of the cart, but when I tried to stand, I was unable to move. My head was firmly attached to the cart. I tried again. Nope. I reached up with my hand to investigate. To my profound irritation, I surmised that the broken piece of the cart that had been clipping me in the knee was now caught in the topknot on my head. My ponytail holder was hooked on the cart, and I could not get it loose. I was bent over, my yoga-pant-clad heinie exposing my folly, with my head fettered to the basket. The toddler in the baby seat was kicking me in the face. Repeatedly.

I pictured myself yelling for help. But in exposing my vulnerability, I feared someone might snatch a baby. While it occurred to me that the babies might indeed be better off, I resolved not to cry for help. But I couldn't reach my purse, which had my cell phone in it. And even if I could have reached it, other than snapping an awesomely awkward selfie for Facebook, whom would I call and what would I say? Trash was blowing past me like I was in a vortex, and the babies started to cry. I tugged and pulled, but I could not break away.

I had only one choice. Hunchbacked, I pushed the basket back into the store *with my head*. I was held so low to the ground by my entangled hair that I was forced to waddle like a duck.

Sam, the three-year-old, kept saying, "Mommy, what you doing?" I ignored him because, well, obviously, I had to keep pushing. The force required for me to push my children, a year's supply of diapers, and the last shred of my dignity was colossal. I tried not to cry. A scorching cyclone of Texas wind blew a mangled Target ad into my downturned face, and I observed that I had been overcharged for the diapers.

The automatic door flew wide, and I collapsed to my knees.

"Are you okay?" asked the greeter at the door.

I sobbed, "No! This basket is caught in my hair!"

She bent over and looked me in the eyes. She was probably a hundred years old. She had apparently taken advantage of the Maybelline sale and was well painted. Hot-pink lipstick was smeared on her aged, wooden-looking teeth, and she smiled a mischievous grin, admonishing, "God love you, you should be more careful."

Indeed.

Tough days seem to outnumber easy days. One of the traps I have fallen into is the belief that these lousy days would entirely cease once I had perfected my walk with God. I continually chalked up the horrible days to my lack of faith. Worse still, I often concluded that anything bad that happened to me was God dishing out judgment on how awful I was. These false beliefs could keep me trapped worse than any shopping cart.

Personality Tests

For so long I obliviously worshipped an idol Jesus who fought the demons of first-world living. Americanized Jesus encourages me to love myself as I am. He tells me self-esteem is the key to happiness, and I should work toward that, work harder to avoid things that hurt or make me feel inadequate. I was trapped in a cycle of philosophies that had to stop for me to advance in my faith walk.

But my failures and misunderstandings cannot impact the Real Jesus. He isn't condescending. He is all about just loving on me and having mercy on me for the ridiculous ways I get tangled up, or whatever it is I find myself caught up in next. Jesus is utterly compassionate.

I spent years trying to gain the love of man and even more years trying to figure out how to make Jesus love me. (I want to be His favorite.) For so much of my life, I have been twisting Jesus into a human character I can identify with. Alas, Jesus is way too complicated to fit into the confines of a personality test.

I have wondered what categories Jesus would fall into if I could sit down and give Him a thorough personality test, like the Myers-Briggs assessment. Perhaps then I would be able to say, "You see there, Jesus, You have a tendency to do that because of Your introverted personality." Alas, He is too grand for our rudimentary psychological exams. He'd be off the charts in every positive way. Discovering the depths of His character is like peeling an onion. New mercies stun me; unanswered prayers mystify me. Yet He moves how He moves, and He saves how He saves, and the greatness of His mystery keeps me yearning for more.

The more I allow Him to be all-in-all instead of trying to make Him fit my brain, the more real He becomes. And this is epic. Because He is everything to everyone—and discovering that He is right where you need Him and how you need Him only increases your understanding of the depths of the Son of Man.

In my quest for Real Jesus, the waters are constantly muddied by the human race. I am always in search of some wise savant to explain God to me. This desire to desperately want all the right answers, and to want them quickly, causes me to fall prey to anyone I think might have those answers. Insecure, I continually seek anyone to tell me how He should be, how I should be, in hopes of discovering the specific protocol for perfection. When my brother-in-law died, I went through Beth Moore's Bible study *Believing God*. When it was over, I was obsessed with…Beth Moore. Granted, she was the catalyst for much healing. However, if I met her and told her that I had become fixated on her, I am certain she'd be offended and hurt to her core. I'd missed the point.

Seeing Jesus through another's eyes can both curse and bless. The pious can render you unable to approach Him. And the lukewarm? They might lead you to believe He couldn't care less.

Looks Can Deceive

Years ago, a mom from playgroup invited me to join a local civic club. I lasted about a year. Once we went on a weekend get-to-know-you retreat at a fancy camp not far from home. At the time, it was a huge treat. I had three little ones, and I was genuinely excited to be getting away, especially with grown-up women friends.

We were split into groups, and my group leader was a woman who looked like a ballerina. She was in her early twenties and had the face of a Madonna, impossibly thick, long auburn hair, catlike jade eyes, and cheekbones to kill for. And she seemed like the rudest, most stuck-up, un-fun person on the planet. As we played puerile games like "I have never" and "Hi, my name is…," she sat back with her arms folded, a revolted scowl on her porcelain face. Everyone in the group was stunned at her attitude. We all ate together, and many of us tried, and failed, to engage her in conversation. She gave short, one-word answers and all but scoffed when we joked or laughed.

The second day one of the members attending the retreat gave us all a personality test and then separated us into the groups by which we were categorized. My stuck-up, un-fun, insolent group leader was left all alone. She had no assembly. She was literally the only person in the group of thirty with her particular disposition. She sat by herself, looking beyond horrified, as the facilitator read aloud the traits of each of the categories. Hers was somewhere between clinically insane and sociopath, and there she sat—all eyes on her. The next activity in her living nightmare was to draw names and discuss what you had learned with the person whose name had been selected. She drew my name. She and I could barely contain our excitement.

We sat and stared at each other. And then I began to ramble, partly because it was awkward, and partly because, as the test had just confirmed, I like the sound of my own voice. Finally, she cracked, and she began to weep. She was in her own private hell. She hated this club, she didn't know anyone, and she wanted to go home. Her mother was a longtime member who had forced her into the organization and then volunteered her to leadership positions. She was a new mom with a four-month-old at home. Her breasts were engorged with milk, and she longed to nurse her baby girl in her own bed. Her husband had told her, as she was leaving for the retreat, that he was being laid off and that they would most likely need to move in with his parents while he looked for a new job.

I asked her if I could pray for her, and she tentatively agreed. I stumbled through a tongue-tied prayer, and then she excused herself and went back into her sequestered world. The retreat came to an end, and I never saw her again.

Trapped. Held hostage by the world, by other people's beliefs about her, by how she felt about others and herself. She bore battle scars from years of social anxiety and fresh wounds from the stark season in her life. And those wounds made her appear cold and uninviting to onlookers. Misunderstood, misinterpreted, and miserable.

I remember the stunning woman wore a simple gold cross. I'd

seen it before and thought about how incongruous it was with the attitude she displayed. *She's a Christian and she acts like that?*

But followers of Jesus are not perfect. Followers of Jesus are just people. Followers of Jesus are a hot mess, sinners all. The tragedy is that believers and nonbelievers alike attribute characteristics of Christians to Christ Himself.

Christians "should be..."

And personally? This is how I developed the psychobabble of the many Jesuses. Let me be very clear: There is one Christ. When I say these names—Target Jesus, Americanized Jesus, High School Jesus—I am conveying the human characteristics placed upon the head of the Son of Man. And all these characters needed to be dismantled for me to see the genuine character of Christ.

That night in my prayer chair, as Stolen Jesus looked up to heaven—or something—I knew it was time to figure this out. I needed to look back to the beginning of my faith (or lack-of-faith) journey. Dread washed over me: This was going to hurt. It might even be agonizing. But much like childbirth, agony would be followed by new life.

The hair tie snaps loose, a flood of blonde curls untangles from the shopping cart and tumbles down my shoulders. I crack my neck from side to side, stand up straight, and look at the face of Truth.

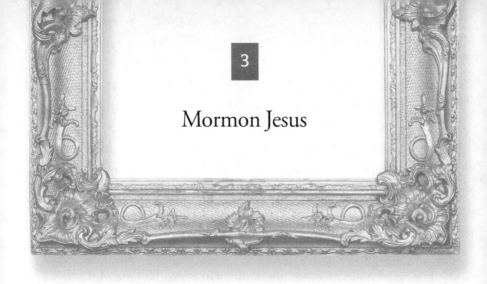

3

Mormon Jesus

Draw near to God, and he
will draw near to you.

JAMES 4:8 ESV

My earliest childhood memory is waiting for my dad to return to our station wagon on the side of the road on some random "shortcut" where we'd once again run out of gas. This is how we rolled, or stalled out, again. I was never specifically taught to hitchhike to the nearest gas station, but if I ever needed to, I could.

My parents loved my younger sister, Stacey, and little brother, Michael, and me. We were very close. Because my dad's job required him to transfer to different areas, we moved a lot—ten or twelve times before I (barely) graduated from high school. I spent a *lot* of my childhood in tents on camping escapades. In my family, camping was not conditional on the weather, just like the gas needle on *E* didn't mean you should stop to refuel. The rest of my youth was spent in hotels as we moved and resettled in each new town on my dad's career path. He worked as a fireman and a motorcycle mechanic to support our family as he steadily made his way through college studying to become a geologist.

My parents are both from Utah. My dad was raised "worshipping" at the base of the Wasatch Front, the mountain range in Ogden, Utah. Camping, fly-fishing, hunting, and motocross were church to him. And like most non-Mormons from Utah, he was firmly anti-religion, especially anti-Mormon religion. I do not remember him ever setting foot inside a Mormon church.

My mom, his high school sweetheart, tried her best to stay the course with her Mormon roots. Some of my earliest memories are of going to our neighborhood ward with my mom, aunt, and cous-ins. (In Utah, you don't visit different Mormon churches to find one you like. You go to the one closest to your home—and there is one on every corner. That's your ward.) My aunt and cousins and neigh-borhood friends were always there. I loved to color printable sheets in Primary—the Mormon after-school program. I remember pic-tures of a man receiving messages from an angel. Later I would learn that the man was Joseph Smith, the founder of the Church of Jesus Christ of Latter-day Saints (Mormons). And we were always given little cubes of green Jell-O as a snack. I loved that the most.

So I was Mormon. And my maternal grandparents were Mor-mon, and my paternal grandparents were anti-Mormon. And my mom's mom, Grandma Jean, was a flamboyant lunatic, and my dad's mom, Grandma Mickey, was sheer perfection.

My Mormon Grandma Jean smoked, which was against the basic moral code of Mormonism, but even worse...*she drank cof-fee*. She would buy Folgers crystals and put them in her Sanka con-tainers—but she wasn't fooling Mormon Jesus.* And even at a very young age, I knew it was a "sin" to drink coffee.

---

* Sanka is a Mormon-approved, non-caffeinated coffee substitute.

I have one particularly vivid memory of Grandma Jean covered in Noxzema, like a clown painted white. Her home-dyed, violet-red hair was standing on end, and bright-red lipstick covered her prim lips. Her false teeth were in a glass of Listerine on the window-sill, and her "garments" (which is the name of the official underwear of the faithful LDS) were spilling out of her *enormous* purple terry-cloth robe. And she was smoking a cigarette, sucking down instant coffee, and wailing-crying.

Wailing-crying was Grandma Jean's trademark. Something to do with shock treatments and an inability to control her emotions. She could cry like she'd just witnessed the slaughter of her forty-nine grandchildren. On this morning, she was wailing-crying about how she couldn't stop drinking coffee and that she was afraid the bishop would find out and she would be excommunicated, and they would have to move to Arizona for the shame. She kept bawl-ing at Grandpa George, whom she called "Daddy," begging him for a solution.

Grandpa George sat at the opposite end of the table, smoking and drinking coffee, and feeding coffee to my baby sister, Stacey, off his spoon while she colored. Neither of them looked at Grandma Jean. I wondered why no one seemed concerned that my baby sis-ter was destined to the lowly first level of heaven, and no higher, for her lackadaisical consumption of creamy java. Every once in a while, Grandpa George would acknowledge my grandma by saying, "Have another cigarette so you can calm down, Jean." And she'd wail, "Jesus, help me!" and have another.

So my earliest conclusions were that Jesus didn't mind if you ate green Jell-O, but He didn't want you to smoke. I knew that cof-fee was bad (but only if you got caught) and that two-year-old Sta-cey was a terrible Mormon. I knew you had to go to your ward. I knew you had to obey the rules of the Mormon Jesus, the Book of

Mormon, *The Doctrine and Covenants*, and *The Pearl of Great Price*, and I knew you had to sneak around. (Grandpa George wasn't a world-class sneak. No one who heard his rattling, tar-filled cough would believe he hadn't been smoking since the third grade.)

I also knew Grandma Jean didn't like me. Once I'd overheard her bawling to my mother, "How can a child as beautiful as Jami be straight from Satan?" In all fairness, I had most recently made a Holy Garment mistake. Grandma Jean had asked me to take the laundry out to the clothesline. I had taken the wrong basket. The basket I left out in the yard held her "garments." Unattended, the size-26 undies could have easily been stolen by a passerby who then could have fraudulently donned them, faking a legitimate temple recommend.* Had the sacred undies been stolen, it would have required another trip to the temple, which she didn't have time for because of dedicated scheduling commitments to the Baptism of the Dead,† choir, the relief society, Bridge Club, and pottery class. Also, Grandpa George already had to drive her to her baptismal commitments at the temple. He would not be interested in making extra trips. Of course, he had to drive her because she wouldn't turn left. (Her theory was that if you turned right enough times it wouldn't ever be necessary to turn left. But the one-way streets in downtown Salt Lake City and Temple Square made the trip an all-day event of turning right.)

Before you get too sad for me, I need to add that Grandma Mickey made up for everything. Grandma Mickey, my dad's mom, made quilts, pies, soups, and tiny hand-sewn teddy bears, each with

---

* A "recommend" is given to members of the Mormon church who have been baptized and confirmed. It also requires an interview with a bishop, who is responsible for determining one's standard of Christlike living.

† Yes, this is real. In the Mormon church, a living person can act as proxy to a dead person and be baptized by immersion on his or her behalf. This supposedly grants the deceased person entry into the kingdom of God.

a personality and an outfit for any occasion. When I played soccer, I got a bear with a uniform like mine. When I danced, the bears had dresses to match my recital costumes. And when I married Justin, there were bears on our wedding cake to match us. In the summer, when we would visit, she set up child-size tables and chairs in her garden. She would give my cousins and me little baskets with delicate napkins she had embroidered, and we would pick the berries that grew along her white picket fence. Along with the juicy fruit, she would serve hand-whipped cream, homemade preserves, and fresh-baked bread.

Unlike Grandma Jean, she enjoyed my company, she didn't assume I was the spawn of Satan, she didn't smoke, she ground her own coffee beans, she never yelled, and she turned left. She even drove a white sports car with red leather seats. But she and Grandpa Don didn't go to their neighborhood ward. Often, I heard my mom's family talk about how tragic this was. This worried me too. Only part of my family attended the Mormon church, and I suspected I knew what that meant would happen to them.

But Grandma Mickey was kind to me. I remember helping her in the garden one day when I was young. Impatient with the process of waiting for the tulips to bloom, I meticulously dug into them and forced open the petals of all of her prized pink and yellow bulbs. Grandma Mickey and Grandpa Don were upset, and they explained to me that I had to let the tulips open on their own. But then they hugged me and told me they loved me.

I said I was sorry. And they said they understood how hard it was to wait for the tulips to open on their own schedule. Grandpa Don and I clipped large pink roses for the table, and then it was over and done. No worries.

I never remember my Grandma Mickey being hysterical, except for two times. Once when they lost their house and everything they owned in a mudslide and another time when my Uncle Richard told her he was marrying a Mormon girl. I was sitting on the kitchen counter; she was washing dishes. My uncle said he was getting married in the temple and that Grandma Mickey and Grandpa Don couldn't come because if they set foot in the temple, it would come tumbling down. She threw a plate. And then she cried.

I recall that I would not have put it past her to rebelliously march into the temple just to watch it collapse, and this scared me too. Why wouldn't she just be Mormon? If she would become a Mormon, she could go to the wedding, the temple wouldn't collapse, and she would also get to go to heaven. Furthermore, she could have some green Jell-O.

I wasn't the only one concerned about my family's entry into heaven. Sometimes, after my parents put us to bed, I would hear voices in the living room and get up to investigate. I would hide and watch as Uncle Denis, my dad's oldest brother, told my parents and a roomful of people about Jesus. He was always holding a Bible, and he talked like the bishop of our ward. But he was talking about a different Jesus, not Mormon Jesus. He talked about "salvation" and "baptism." I heard him tell a story—I don't know if it's true or not—about how the only reason Mormons couldn't have coffee was that the founder of the church, Joseph Smith, got into a fight with the traders and couldn't get coffee imported. So Smith lied and said that God told him that Mormons couldn't drink coffee anymore.

Shortly after that, my father graduated from Weber State College with a degree in geology. He was hired by an oil company, and another leg of our nomadic life began. We moved to Farmington, New Mexico, and then Houston, Texas. We no longer attended wards. We participated in the Assembly of God. And there was loud music, and people put their hands in the air and sang and spoke in different languages. Sadly, there were no more cubes of green Jell-O.

My mom and dad got baptized in a mysterious pool behind the pulpit. And midway through the long services, we all got little crackers and grape juice.

While unpacking our apartment in Houston, my mom got a letter in the mail. I heard her tell my dad that she and I had been excommunicated from the Mormon church because we ate the crackers and grape juice at the Assembly of God. It has long been assumed that Grandma Jean told the bishop what we had done while asking his advice on getting us back into the Mormon church. But the news of our excommunication for apostasy horrified her.

What was especially peculiar was the inclusion of my name on the letter. At the time I wasn't old enough to have been baptized into the church, and officially only baptized Mormons can be excommunicated. I remember seeing the letter on the table, neatly typed and folded, with a picture of the Salt Lake City temple on the header.*

I was confused. And I thought Jesus was probably mad, but I couldn't figure out why. I knew the rule about the coffee; I knew Stacey couldn't be Mormon because of the sips from Grandpa George's spoon. However, I couldn't believe Mormons couldn't eat crackers and drink grape juice. I could have sworn that had been okay.

After Houston, my dad was transferred back to Farmington. A few months after we settled into our third house in two years, Grandpa George passed away in his sleep. Then *everyone* wailed hysterically. And if my mom had any ties left to the Mormon church, they were permanently severed when two men in suits arrived at

* While writing this chapter, my mother and I went on the hunt for the letter she received all those years ago—proof of our "apostasy" and excommunication. Alas, the many moves have led to losses here and there, and we've been unable to find the letter. I also attempted to research church records regarding myself and my family. Genealogy is important because the church believes families will be united for eternity. (This is also the basis for baptism and tithing for the dead.) Unfortunately, I was unable to locate records for myself, my mother, and two of my aunts. This was not surprising: Because the Mormon church believes in ongoing prophetic changes, documents are often changed, amended, or destroyed.

Grandma Jean's house a few days after the funeral. They informed her that Grandpa George had been behind in his tithes to the church. She would have to pay his back tithes, or he wouldn't be in heaven and they couldn't be together for eternity.

Grandma Jean signed over every penny of his meager life insurance and lived on insufficient funds the rest of her days.

The rest of my youth was shrouded in a true distaste for all things Mormon. My mom was frank about the danger of believing in an earned salvation. But my family was still my family. When a cousin left on a mission* or was made bishop, we heard about it through the grapevine.

The family was anxious about us, of course—we'd lost eternal life. "Oh my heck, they aren't Mormon?" (Excuse my Utahan.) And I was just as anxious about them and their salvation. Jesus seemed so complicated to me. Who was right? Who was wrong? Why would He take an old lady's money, especially when she was so sad? And what in the name of Joseph Smith was wrong with crackers and grape juice?

Questions like this and my parents' distaste for all things LDS left me curious about religion, God, green Jell-O, and grape juice. And so, many years later, sitting in my prayer chair under the watchful gaze of Stolen Jesus, I wondered why the bad stuff is the stuff that sticks the hardest. Grandma Jean's Mormon Jesus was harsh and unforgiving. Mormon Jesus thought I was the spawn of the devil. And apparently Mormon Jesus only cared that I followed the rules if someone was watching.

That Jesus will make you hysterical. But I was becoming more confident. I was realizing that Mormon Jesus wasn't the Real Jesus.

---

* Every "worthy" young Mormon man is called to devote himself to two years of missionary service when he turns eighteen.

He was just a manifestation Satan used to keep me far from the truth.

All my young life—even during those years in the ward—I'd had an inexplicable and curious love for Jesus. I always knew He was real, knew He was present (although it would be years before I embraced His magnificence). But people and circumstances can negatively influence our opinions of Jesus. Just like girls with lousy daddies sometimes have trouble grasping the overwhelming love of a Father in heaven, I had unfairly associated a negative Jesus with poor Grandma Jean and the Mormon church.

Grandma Jean, I should say here, was not all bad. Her commitment to her Noxzema regimen afforded her the softest skin on the planet. She wrote typed letters, in ALL CAPS, and she ended every sentence with an exclamation point. This made even the simplest notes ooze with excitement! "DEAR JAMI! HAPPY BIRTHDAY! I HOPE YOU LIKE YOUR SOCKS! I WENT TO THE STORE IN OGDEN TO GET THEM! IT IS SNOWING HERE! I AM OUT OF NOXEMA!"

And that is how she lived—with uninhibited emotion for things that were sad and things that were happy. She decided to get her GED when she was in her late sixties just so she could say she had finished high school. She never forgot a birthday or anniversary, and she made a mean macaroni salad.

And yet she was constantly destabilized by her roller-coaster emotions. I believe she wanted nothing more than peace. But the things that brought her some level of peace—coffee, cigarettes, and shock treatments—were the very things that made her mad with fear and guilt. I fully believe that this is another one of the devil's most devious games. The whisper: "Jesus isn't enough. Your faith isn't sufficient. If you really loved Him, if you really trusted Him, you wouldn't need Zoloft."

I don't think Jesus is caught off guard by the advancements in modern medicine. Do you question the faith of someone who is suffering from bronchitis? Or a yeast infection? Nope. You tell them to take an antibiotic or get some Monistat. If there is a voice that chastises and mocks you when you need assistance, be leery. It is a very distinct sound, and it is laced with condemnation and harshness. I know now that's not Real Jesus. There is another voice that only wants you to be well. That voice might nudge you in a direction away from a medicinal fix. Or it might be serene and wise like Grandpa George: "Have another to calm yourself."

Jesus doesn't want you in hysterics. I think He would much rather you have a Xanax than be tased by the TSA and arrested for a crazed assault on an air marshal. Sometimes the outside influences that tell us we aren't working hard enough in our faith drown out the voice of Jesus saying, *Baby, this is the help you've been asking for.* The more layers of lies that fell off of my beliefs about Jesus, the more confident I became to say, "I love Jesus, and sometimes I need a prescription."

From my chair, I lifted an eyebrow at Stolen Jesus. "Do you care if I drink coffee?" I asked.

He didn't respond.

So I went and got a cup, and I toasted it to Grandma Jean.

God love you, woman. You were doing the best you could.

4

Fifth-Grade Jesus

I keep asking that the God of our Lord
Jesus Christ, the glorious Father, may give
you the Spirit of wisdom and revelation,
so that you may know him better.

EPHESIANS 1:17

In 2001, our oldest, Maggie, was in first grade, and I was staying home with John and Luke and pregnant with Sophie. One day Maggie came home from school with a note about elementary girls' softball. The letter from the coach said he hoped Maggie would join the team. I read over it and thought, *Good parents do this for their kids. They let them play softball.*

I gave the note to Justin at dinner, and we began to discuss it. I didn't want her to miss out on this experience all the other girls were having, I said. Miss Maggie, six-year-old sass, piped up: "I am NOT playing softball."

To which Justin, without missing a lick, said, "You will NOT tell us what you will and won't do! You are playing." He hauled her to the car, and they went and bought a glove, bat, and ball and started practicing that night. She cried, he yelled, I ordered softball pants, and the next Tuesday night we loaded up and went to softball.

Maggie stunk. She picked flowers in the outfield. Justin paced. I chased John and Luke. I wanted to chat with the other mommies, but those boys were all over the place. I was fat, pregnant, and sweaty. Softball in West Texas is the armpit of sporting. The wind blew, and with it the dirt and pollen.

We braved it for three weeks. After the third weekly practice, we dragged our filthy family home. I gave halfhearted baths and muddled through Maggie's spelling list. We managed to make some grilled cheese sandwiches. I got my bath and limped into bed.

Justin rolled in next to me. His pajamas were a little wet—he was too tired to even dry off from his shower. He whimpered, "What were we thinking? She hates softball. I hate softball. Why are we doing this?"

I whined, "Because she said she wouldn't." But at the same time, I knew it was also because I just wanted to do what everyone else was doing.

Justin moaned, "I can't do this. What are we going to do?"

And it came to me like manna from heaven: "Let's pretend it never happened!" And Justin perked up to listen to my diabolical plan.

We would get rid of all softball evidence. I threw away the schedule that was on the fridge, tossed the shirt, pants, hat, glove, ball, and bat. We would literally make it all disappear and never speak of it again. If Maggie were to ask about it, we would either ignore her or treat her like she was crazy. Voilà! No more softball.

Well, Maggie's disdain for the game bought us two weeks. And then, one night at dinner, she said, "Katie said they missed me at the softball game Saturday. How come we didn't go?"

Stay cool, stay cool. Justin cleared his throat. "What softball game?" Maggie looked at him and chirped, "Remember? You made me play softball? I have a red T-shirt? We go to the softball park next to the lake?"

Justin was going to blow it, I could tell. So I reached for my iced tea and knocked it over. Chaos. Perfect. As I mopped up the mess, I casually said, "Hmm, Mags, maybe you dreamed that. You and your witty imagination." She looked a little confused, but I quickly changed the subject. "Speaking of your imagination, did you show Daddy the picture you drew? I put it on the fridge." You see what I did there? She went to the fridge and got the picture, and there was no softball schedule...just her artwork. Brilliant. (Judge me all day long if you'd like. Maggie is all grown up and attending college in Oxford, England. She turned out fine.)

So we were never to speak of this again. We went on with our lives, and we were all the better for having quit softball without being quitters.

All was well and good until the end-of-the-year ceremonies at the school. We headed to the school, camcorder in hand, and listened proudly as Maggie and her class sang some catchy oldies and recited a little Robert Frost. Then the awards ceremony began. I think Maggie got a good citizenship award and a little medal for sitting with a new kid at lunch. Pride swelled. And then, *Oh no oh no oh no...he* stood up with a box full of little trophies.

I jabbed Justin in the ribs. He looked at me, completely clueless, and mouthed, "What?"

And then he saw what I had seen.

It was the softball coach.

So, in an ordinary society, if you stop showing up for a sport three weeks after it began, you do not get a trophy for your participation.

But this is America, folks, and everyone gets an award. And of course, let's go in alphabetical order. He began, and surely everyone in the cafeteria-auditorium could hear my heart pounding.

And "Our first trophy goes to outfielder"—seriously, how far *out*-field did they think she had been?—"Maggie Amerine!" Applause. Maggie walked to the podium and took her little trophy, eyeing Justin and me the entire way there and back, brown eyes searing a hole through our souls, and then she mouthed at us, "I KNEW I PLAYED SOFTBALL."

She still has that silly trophy. I confess we did try this brainwashing method one other time—*only* one other time—with a dead parakeet. I mean, what parakeet? We never had a parakeet. But at the root of this folly (okay, okay, aside from lousy parenting) is the lie that I need to be like everyone else and do what everyone else is doing. My kids need to be dressed, pressed, fully enveloped in the madness and acting like everyone around them. These urgings keep me frazzled, exhausted, and waddling around a lake chasing lunatic toddlers in gale-force West Texas winds, and for what? How does this bring God glory? How does this bring me closer to the Real Jesus?

There are many robbers of joy in this fallen world, but I believe the first is to measure my worth by the world's standards of appearance. The second is to try and be something you are not. This place of judgment and envy is where I continually miss out on the wonder of Real Jesus. Coveting or obsessing over how someone else lives and breathes is one of the enemy's most simple-minded tricks. I wish I could tell you that I learned something from the softball experience, but alas, I still covet the Joneses. I work hard to keep up with them.

On that night in the living room, I had to come to terms with why I believed I had to be someone other than the girl God created me to be. Why did I compare myself to other people, wanting desperately to be liked and accepted? I had to look intently at why I needed to fit in at all costs. And as painful as it was going to be, I knew that meant it was time to come face-to-face with Fifth-Grade Jesus.

As a young child in school, I struggled academically and socially. Later I would be diagnosed with learning disabilities, but at the time I was just labeled "difficult." I don't remember being difficult. Distracted, bored, fidgety? Sure. But, at my core, I wanted teachers and other students to like me, which they did not. I remember being left out and lonely.

We moved to Abilene, Texas, when I was in fourth grade. I had a teacher I adored, but mid-semester she received an adoption placement after years of waiting, and she left. In her departure, she abandoned me to a wicked woman named Ms. Drummond.

Ms. Drummond terrorized anyone who didn't make straight As. This teacher was the stuff nightmares are made of. As wide as she was tall, bleach-blonde, 1950s beehive hairdo, and coffee breath. She called me by my full name, complete with a West Texas drawl, "Jami-Jo MACELVEEE." I tried to correct her one time ("Ms. Drummond, my last name is McKelvie. Mick, not Mac"), and she gave me recess detention for a week for being disrespectful.

The rest of the year wasn't much better. As a capstone to the nightmare, the last day of school I threw up on the bus ride home in front of all my peers and the beautiful Nick Gerrard, with whom I was utterly smitten. He yelled at me, "EW! You splashed barf on my Kappas! You freak!" The stress of the school year and the icky sweets we'd gorged ourselves on at the end-of-the-year bash had crept back up on me. I barely had any warning. The bus driver glared at me, the other kids gagged and clawed to get away from me, and I was humiliated and ready to move to a different city.

Luckily, my dad already had a transfer in hand to Victoria, Texas. The move to Victoria started out terribly. We couldn't find a house, so we spent months at the La Quinta hotel. The diner attached to the hotel was breakfast, lunch, and dinner. And in a freak accident involving a spill, my sister, Stacey, was severely burned in the restaurant. With no friends or family in town and my parents keeping vigil at the burn unit with Stacey, Michael and I were stuck in the hotel for hours at a time.

After two months we found a house, a nurse from the hospital invited us to her church, and we were back in the swing of things. My mom made a good friend who had a daughter going into the fifth grade. Haley was sweet, beautiful, and famous in our neighborhood. Haley and her family had a slumber party to introduce me to all the other fifth-grade girls, and the next day the entire fifth-grade class came over to swim. I had a gang. I had friends and a church.

One night while I was sleeping over at Haley's, her mom came in and prayed with us before we went to sleep. She thanked God for me and praised Him for sending me to Victoria, Texas. I fell asleep with a grin on my face. The following Sunday I accepted Jesus as my Savior, and the Sunday after that I got baptized in the mysterious bathtub behind the place where the pastor spoke. I can't remember ever being so happy, except at my Grandma Mickey's. And then...

It was time to register for school. This school was concerned with my grades, which had been transferred from Abilene, and as an added bonus, Ms. Drummond had added a long letter to my transcript about how I was "disrespectful, obnoxious, and unpleasant." I saw the note when the counselor took my mom into the hall to "chat."

I knew those things were not true of me. I could feel a tightness in my throat, my eyes burned, my heart pounded. They returned and tried to gently explain that I would not be in the fifth grade—that it was essential for me to repeat the fourth grade.

When we got back to the house, Haley and two of the other fifth-grade girls were waiting for me, sitting on their bikes on the front porch of my house. The minute we came around the corner, I could see the purple flag that was attached to the impeccably white banana seat of Haley's hot-pink Schwinn bike.

My heart accelerated with reprieve. I would tell them the horrors of the meeting and the evil plot of Ms. Drummond, fourth-grade criminal mastermind, to extinguish my hopes and dreams. I couldn't wait to pour my heart out to them, to weep my frustrations to my newfound "sisters in Christ." All the terms were new to me, but the warm, fuzzy feelings associated with them made me confident that I would still have my gang, and we would get through this together with a little prayer and Jesus.

I was wrong.

That was the last conversation I had with Haley. None of the fifth graders ever spoke to me again. At church, I was moved to the fourth-grade Sunday school class. To say I was humiliated would be the understatement of the year.

Fifth-grade Sunday school participants read the actual Bible, and I had a brand-new Bible that my parents presented to me at my baptism. We were supposed to bring highlighters and a blue pen to makes notes in the margin. I already had a chambray bag with fluorescent piping and a *J* embroidered on the front that Grandma Mickey had made in celebration of my baptism. She had stocked it full of pens with fuzzy balls on top, a package of highlighters, a fluorescent-green spiral notebook, and a book of *Ghostbusters* stickers.

Fourth-grade Sunday school had coloring sheets of Zacchaeus up a tree. They sang "Jesus Loves Me." The supply list for fourth-grade Sunday school was a twenty-four-count box of crayons, a box of animal crackers, and a bottle of apple juice to share with the class.

Fourth grade seemed to last a decade rather than a nine-month stint where I would perfect cursive and try and fail again at mastering long division. Haley's mom was super friendly to me, but it was laced with obvious pity. She tried to make Haley talk to me once, but Haley leaned over and whispered to her friend Karen and skipped away. And I don't blame Haley or any of the other fifth-grade girls, but I created a new Jesus: Fifth-Grade Jesus.

Fifth-Grade Jesus is all about achievement. He likes girls and boys who make straight As. They don't get held back. They are in His clique—brothers and sisters in Christ. They have a certain level of perfection that I assumed you were born with. At this point in my faith walk, all I knew for sure was I couldn't catch up with the Jesus I had briefly experienced before I was held back.

Back in my prayer chair, safe in my grown-up world, Stolen Jesus quietly stared back at me as I sobbed and wrote story after story of feeling left out, alone, and desperate to fit in at each new school. The debacles were laughable, but I wasn't ready to laugh. And I knew it wasn't going to get much better, as I was about to have a reunion with High School Jesus. But there in the prayer chair, I wrote out every single lie I believed about Fifth-Grade Jesus. I asked Real Jesus to show me the truth about how He felt about me that day. I asked Him if Ms. Drummond was right about me. I asked Him to pour out blessings on Haley and all of the fifth graders and Ms. Drummond. I knew those words didn't come from me. But I let them come, and I let go of years of hurt.

Real Jesus was uncovering His character, bringing light to the dark places.

5

High School Jesus

*What goes into someone's mouth does
not defile them, but what comes out of
their mouth, that is what defiles them.*

MATTHEW 15:11

Somewhere in the chemistry of the Americanized teen-being, there is a biological warfare being waged that causes a kid to fluctuate between normalcy and unadulterated psychosis. We recently came to terms with the reality that the second batch of children we have invited into our home and given our last name to will enter the teens about the time we are in our late fifties. Our goal is not to be on *Dateline*: "Family Slaughtered by Band of Orphans." Or "Teens Slaughtered by Crazed Parents."

We homeschooled, raised chickens, read Lewis and Tolkien, memorized scriptures, and ate organic spinach. We thought we had the formula for perfection. Still, there is a point when babies start to toddle, toddlers become children, and children becomes raging lunatics. They just do. E-mail me about your perfect teen, and I'll hire a camera crew to come over and record your demise. They just have to sprout, and they don't always sprout altogether well.

Shazam! Like a light switch, one day you have a twelve-year-old daughter who sings praise-and-worship songs while she mindfully unloads the dishwasher with your foster baby on her hip. The next day she blows thirteen candles out on her My Little Pony cake and *BAM!* She starts wearing all black, cries if you ask her to brush her hair, and asks if she can get a tramp stamp tattoo with her birthday money. The next morning, she comes to breakfast in a pink sundress with a giant yellow hair bow reading *Little House on the Prairie*. By dinner, she's back in black, asking if you can please order her a black velvet cape off Amazon. She proceeds to tell you she wants to demonstrate her disdain for the government and her desire to exhibit her hatred by dressing in the "cloak of darkness" that is suppressing the less fortunate.

No worries, tomorrow she will come to breakfast in a full-length skirt with a collared shirt buttoned to her neck and a bun in her hair, begging you to please sign a permission slip so she can play the oboe in the junior high band. And so it goes. The identity crisis is a real struggle, my friends. And the crisis in this generation is far beyond that which we thought we would encounter even five years ago. Technology makes the pursuit of innocence so much harder.

My best advice is to make no sudden movements. Just roll with it. In all fairness, I was a train wreck as a teen. Which brings me to the prayer chair, in the middle of the night, coming face-to-face with High School Jesus.

My family moved on from Victoria, but we didn't find a new church in the next few moves. Life got busier and harder. The oil economy crashed, and my dad was laid off for a season. By the time I was a sophomore in high school, we landed back in Abilene, Texas.

Joy.

Seeing as I had such a positive experience there the first time, I was less than excited to return. (This, you'll recall, was the land of Ms. Drummond, my fourth-grade nemesis.) Lucky for me, I hadn't had a single friend when I left the first time. In some ways, it was a fresh start. But new girls in small towns, where the kids have been together since kindergarten, are not exactly welcomed with open arms, especially if those new girls are tall and blonde. The boys were nice, which only made things worse with the girls.

High school was rough. Scholastically and socially, I was a moron. I made straight Ds. Sometimes I made D+s. I was in the "special" history class where we watched *Bill and Ted's Excellent Adventure* every day and copied vocabulary words out of a history book from the early 1950s. I was in remedial English. (Seeing as I spoke English, I thought I should have at least been in a regular class for that.) My senior year the other kids were reading *The Grapes of Wrath*. My remedial class wasn't "allowed" to read a book of this magnitude. So, while my fellow seniors did research papers on great works of literature, I did mine on Judy Blume's *Are You There God? It's Me, Margaret.* I got a D-.

I was on the school newspaper, which I loved, and I like to think I helped bring the paper to a new level. Through someone my mom knew at work, I organized a campaign to get the paper professionally printed like an actual newspaper. And unbeknownst to anyone, I woke at 6:00 a.m. every morning and watched Jane Pauley and Bryant Gumbel deliver the news. I was current on world events, and I had a journal that had a list of things I would accomplish before I was twenty-five.

1. Read *The Grapes of Wrath*.

2. Finish college with a degree in journalism.

3. Move to New York.

4. Replace Jane Pauley.

The one thing that got me out of bed every morning was that school newspaper. I loved it. It lit a fire in me. The writing and the production were more than a class. I had a purpose. And if I had stuck to the parameters of my assignments, I might have had some real successes.

If only.

It all started at a party—a party to which I was not invited. The boy I was dating brought me anyway. The welcoming committee, which consisted of four girls, was less than cordial. The gang of teen-aged trendsetters had bangs that were shellacked five inches tall with Aqua Net. They wore acid-washed denim skirts and a matching assortment of fluorescent sweatshirts that they'd cut off to expose their midriffs. They were also heavily decorated with massive white plastic jewelry. Their hoop earrings could have doubled as life-saving devices should anyone fall in the pool. Dark-blue eye shadow, electric-blue mascara, and hot-pink lipstick covered their perfectly pimpled faces. Their hatred for me oozed out of their Clearasil-pickled pores.

I don't know what about me bothered them. I was dressed exactly like them. I was funny. Well, I acted like a ditzy blonde and cracked everyone up, but the truth was they were laughing at me, not with me. The modish quad giggled, whispered, and pointed. And I heard words like *slut* and *retard*. I clung to the fact that they didn't know me. I stayed close on the heels of my boyfriend, who was a jerk, but my only ride home. At one point in the nightmarish evening, I made my way to the master suite to use the bathroom.

One of the wicked band of hostesses was holding back the hair of another as she heaved red Everclear Jell-O shots into a fancy mauve-colored toilet. They shot evil glares my way, and I excused myself and went to find another bathroom. I found one—and my boy-friend and a cheerleader from a rival school making out on the country-blue carpeted floor.

Ewww.

I will never understand carpet in bathrooms.

I wandered out onto the porch. Some guy I'd never seen before was collecting money and passing out baggies of what appeared to be pills or pink and blue candies to a mass of greedy teenagers. They ignored me. I wondered how I would get home; I wished I had friends. I sat on the stairs of the mini-mansion, and then suddenly everyone else moved inside as if I was actually that repulsive. My house was about ten miles out of town, in the country, so I wouldn't be walking. I thought about calling my parents, and in hindsight that would have been a better choice. Instead, a boy from another school walked out to get in his truck, and I asked him for a ride.

About a mile from my house he asked me if I had gas money. I didn't, so he pulled over and tried to get something else. He failed, and he walked with a limp for several days. The fight earned me a sprained wrist, a busted lip, and skinned knees from my fall from his truck. Oh, and a terrifying walk home. Coyotes howled at a sliver of moon. The chilly wind made the mesquite trees clatter, and my porch light was the only beacon leading me home. Every single hor-ror flick played out in my mind. I sprinted the rest of the way.

I made it. I went into my parents' room and climbed between them in their white lacquer and brass waterbed and dreamed of New York and Jane Pauley. I drifted to sleep, safe between my mom and dad, relieved that the evening hadn't ended much, much worse.

The next morning my mom announced we were visiting a church. Despite everyone's complaints, an hour later we were walk-ing into the enormous assembly. Every single one of the kids from the night before lined the pews. They whispered and pointed at me. It would be Monday before I learned the story being told by my perverted chauffeur—a story much different from mine. In a strange twist of poetic injustice, his version of the ride home caused my boyfriend to break up with me in a note with *Whore* scribbled across the front.

As the morning erupted with the hypocrisy of worship, the band of haters held hands high and sang "Amazing Grace." They cried and hugged during communion. Their parents crossed aisles, and they embraced. The adults were oblivious to the toxic levels of deceit. The Jell-O Shot Vomiter got up and read a few scriptures. A couple of others circled up to pray over the football team—safe travels and success for their upcoming game. And Fifth-Grade Jesus graduated from His high horse to an even higher pedestal where He sat and judged losers like me.

Evidently, to understand the love of Jesus, you had to be a full-blown jerk. You could sneak around, use Ecstasy, lie, cheat, and be downright nasty as long as you were in church on Sunday. My throat burned from the bile that rose. I hated these people. I hated this church. I hated Jesus.

To add to the offense, on Monday morning a letter was taped inside my locker. Apparently, this band of self-righteous idiots was meeting early on Monday mornings before school to pray for their classmates. There was a list of twenty students who they felt needed prayer more than most. So they had printed up the list and taped it in each of our lockers and titled it "Heaven's Most Wanted." I was number three. This was the highest rank I had achieved in my academic career thus far. Across the hall, I saw a young freshman begin to weep. She was number one.

Indignant, I marched into the counselor's office and began to unleash three years' worth of noxious scorn for the school, faculty, staff, lunch choices, and students. When I was done, the counselor sent me to the principal's office. A teacher drove me home. Rebellion coursed through my teenage veins. And so, I wrote.

I wrote a piece for the school newspaper. My fingers raced across the 8-bit Commodore 64. The dot matrix printer whirled out magic from the wide, clunky carriage turning my words to faded gray print on tractor-fed legal-size paper. I didn't sleep a wink.

The next day I marched into the administration office and shoved my draft toward the man in charge. The administration had to approve all articles before they went to print. The title of what I thought would be a Pulitzer prize–winning piece was "What You Don't Want to See: The Drug and Alcohol Problem Right Under Your Nose." My tight mousse-scrunched hair, inflexible bangs, and shoulder pads were the only things that didn't deflate during this encounter.

First, I was informed that the article would not be run. It was slander. There was no place in real journalism for lies and the rantings of a jaded seventeen-year-old "girl." Second, if I didn't stop spreading rumors about my classmates—classmates who attended the same church as this administrator and his family—I would no longer be allowed to work on the school paper.

Finally, his tone changing to one of pity, he asked me if I had ever considered trying to get my GED. I should look into cosmetology school, he said—I was "such a pretty girl," and I was "dragging down the class average" with my low test scores and terrible GPA.

Behind him on a filing cabinet was a framed copy of the Lord's Prayer.

I hated that man, his school, his church, his congregation, and his Jesus. I was tired of being humiliated. My heart pounded in my ears. I couldn't swallow—the lump in my throat ached and grew. In spite of my desperate attempts to stop it, a tear escaped. I imagined blue mascara on my cheek. He offered me a Kleenex. I ignored him.

He kept the folder with my investigative report and excused me to algebra class. Which was punishment in itself.

In the main office, I saw the girl who had been number one on the list. She was with her mom, and she was crying. She was withdrawing from school, pregnant. She couldn't have been more than fifteen years old. I was sad for her. That stupid school had beat her. Awkwardly, she and I ended up at our lockers at the same time. She unloaded her belongings into a brown box. Sniffling, obviously heartbroken.

One of the girls from the prayer group, Kate, saw the broken freshman weepily cleaning out her locker and said, "Dropping out?"

The freshman nodded.

"Knocked up?" Kate mocked.

She nodded again.

"Slut," Kate chirped, smearing Bonnie Bell lip shine on her hypocritical mouth.

Two weeks later, Kate mysteriously disappeared for the rest of the year, absent from graduation, although rumor had it she ended up being number nine on the prayer list, she and her newborn daughter.

Vengeance is mine, saith High School Jesus.

I withdrew further from anything related to God and religion. I trudged through the rest of the year. The only bright point was when the vice principal, an astute, kind man, and the only guy at the school I liked, handed me a little book.

It was a Friday afternoon, and he stopped me as I was headed out to work-study. He only said, "I want you to have this, Jami." The sweet little worn antique book had an embossed cover that said *I Dare You*. I thanked him and rushed off to work. Later that evening, alone in my room, I thumbed through it. The book, written by William H. Danforth, was printed in 1945. Inside the cover, neatly typed, was written, "PRIVATELY PRINTED FOR MY PERSONAL FRIENDS

AND DARING YOUTH WHO MAY CROSS MY PATH." And this vice principal had sought me out and given the copy to me.

The fourfold development was based on "think tall, smile tall, live tall, and stand tall." None of which I did, but I was now going to. The dares inside were dares to be adventurous, strong, creative, develop a magnetic personality, build character, share, and launch into the deep. What that man did for me at that moment gave me the drive to stay the course. I read the chapters and made a notebook to answer the questions and devised a plan to be successful in spite of my many failures. I held up my chin and pressed on toward the end of the year.

At an award banquet, two of the "ick clique" got "Up and Coming" journalist awards and accolades for their efforts to get the newspaper on newsprint. I got nothing. Cheesecake was served for dessert; they ran out before they reached me at the end of the table. The waiter brought me a peppermint; it looked like it had been sucked on already. My life was like an atrocious Aaron Spelling after-school special. At one point during the banquet, I looked up, and there was that vice principal. He nodded, winked, and gave me a thumbs-up. And I trudged on.

Back then, I had minimally tried to recognize that someone can look fabulous on the outside and be in shambles on the inside. Something can seem like a grand idea—and end up a colossal disaster. I would like to think I have learned I must not seek or measure my joy based on what is seen with the eyes. Looking back, I realize that High School Jesus formulated much that was wrong in my beliefs.

I know now that the ick clique from high school was probably just as pathetic as I was. The first time this occurred to me was at my husband's high school reunion. There were only fifty kids in his graduating class. He always talked about how much fun they had together, and I was jealous of the good times they shared. And then I met his friends. While the guys were reminiscing about the good old days, the girls inserted, "It was a living nightmare."

I knew the ick clique would probably say the same. There are many thieves of peace in this fallen world, but time and again I find that my first enemy is the temptation to measure my world by the standards of appearance, and the second is trying to be something I'm not. This place of judgment and envy is where I continually miss out on the wonder of Real Jesus's loving and kind companionship. Coveting or obsessing over how someone else lives and breathes is one of the enemy's most simpleminded tricks.

The morning of graduation the principal called my mom and said I could walk across the stage, but that I would need to take algebra again over the summer to earn my diploma. However, in a last-ditch effort to rid themselves of me, the algebra teacher found a way to bring my grade up two tenths of a point, and I was finally done. Two days after graduation, I moved to a Girl Scout camp to be a counselor for the summer.

As I left for camp, I was increasingly jaded about religion and God. I professed a love for Jesus, but I was lying. I didn't love Him, or like Him, or know Him. *I Dare You* was my spiritual compass. I set lofty goals I had no way of achieving except by sheer determination. Like the mean girls from my high school, I used Jesus when I was behaving nastily. He was a brand—verbiage I used to maneuver about the Bible Belt. I was a "Christian" who poorly represented the Risen Christ, and I copyrighted Jesus as mighty to save when I needed something or I wanted to hear myself talk and sound wise.

I was an idiot. But I was done with high school, and I was ready for a new adventure. I wanted to fulfill my list of goals. *I Dare You* encouraged me to write them down and claim them as definite rather than probable. I would look in the mirror and with my best news anchor voice say, "You are going to gear up your mind to capacity and share its strength with others. Instead of diminishing by sharing, you will grow immensely strong."

If only. If only we knew then what we know now. Alas, where would I be without the bumps and bruises? In a recent radio interview, John Vonhof of the Writers & Authors on Fire podcast asked me when I knew I wanted to be a writer. I spontaneously chirped, "I didn't!" Which, in that moment, was true. I had forgotten all about my dreams of being a famous journalist.

The night I sat in front of Stolen Jesus, as story after story poured from my fingers, it dawned on me how ugly I had become and how far from my real self I fell after high school. *Jaded*, I guess, is the best way to describe it.

Not until I started the Real Jesus journal did I actually start to write again. And those pages were filled with so much grief. My fingers could barely keep up with the abundance of words that exploded from my broken heart. I wished I could have pulled the "you never played softball" trick on myself. However, not facing it doesn't make it not so. The hard work of mourning the lies and memories of High School Jesus and dismantling Him took longer than I would like to admit. And in the midst of the hard work of letting go, more and more pieces of my made-up Jesuses appeared and fell away.

It was at the Girl Scout camp that I met my friend Lisa. I think she was the first real friend I'd had since kindergarten. We laughed and talked, and she took me home with her on weekends that the camp was closed. She introduced me to her friends, and I finally had a gang.

Toward the end of the summer, my parents announced they were moving again. I decided not to go with them.

Lisa asked me to be her college roommate, although at first I was unable to get into the college she was attending. This school was not in Abilene. It had a journalism program. And I was determined to get in and be successful on my own. A misunderstood and hateful Jesus was tagging along for the ride, and *I Dare You* was in the front pocket of my suitcase.

My newest mantra from my tattered pseudo bible: "Why dare? Because unless you dare you cannot win. Deep down in every heart is the desire to be somebody, to get somewhere. But so often we sit waiting for the opportunity. I have found opportunities do not come to those who wait. They are captured by those who attack."[1] I would attack the future, and I would have fame and fortune. I would not settle for anything less.

The book suggested that the complete person presented a four-square model of mental, social, physical, and religious character. I was eager to check off all four of those boxes. I knew I was mentally determined, and I finally had a real social life. To conquer the physical character, I started teaching aerobics, leg warmers and all.

That left only religion.

If religion meant embracing the Jesuses I believed I'd encountered, I wasn't interested. But yoga seemed to fulfill that mandate. So, I peacefully meditated. I pondered my existence. I was an intellectual, not a dingbat. I was writing my own success story. I attempted to read *The Grapes of Wrath* and hated it, so I deemed it boring and crossed it off my list. I was in control! I enrolled in a couple of remedial classes at the junior college near the university, taught aerobics, and worked at the mall. I felt grown up.

One weekend that fall we went back home to Lisa's house to see friends. Lisa's mom and her mom's identical twin sister were sitting in the living room talking when we walked into the house. Lisa introduced me to her aunt, and the twins started to echo, "Oh, Lisa! Take Jami out to the farm so Justin can look at her! He must see her!" Lisa giggled and herded me back out to the car to be ogled by her cousin.

On the drive, I begged, "I really don't want to meet anyone, Lisa." I was liberated, and I wasn't interested in wrestling with another stupid boy.

She grinned. "It's not like you're going to marry him."

I snorted, "Right. With my luck, I'll end up married to him with seven kids." She laughed, and as we pulled up the dirt driveway Justin stepped out onto the porch. And I knew right then—

I was going to marry him.

6

Justin's Jesus

In my distress I called to the LORD; I
cried to my God for help. From his
temple he heard my voice; my cry
came before him, into his ears.

PSALM 18:6

Justin was a senior in college and worked at the university ranch. He genuinely wore faded Wranglers, unlike the dime-store cowboys you see around these parts. He dressed in snap-front denim work shirts, his boots were ragged and tattered, and he was an absolute dream. He was just as smitten with me. For our first date, we went out for Mexican food and watched Steven King's *Children of the Corn*. He dropped me off at my apartment and called me as soon as he got home. Two weeks later I cooked him chicken-fried pheasant, wild rice, and green beans with slivered almonds. He was hungry, surviving on fried bologna and white bread, so he asked me to marry him.

But more than hungry for a decent meal, he was my friend. He laughed with me, not at me. He opened doors for me and told me I was gorgeous. He winked at me and called me "punkin'" and "blondie" with a soft Texas drawl. And he said things like, "You're so smart! I never thought of that!" And I believed him. For the first time in my life, I believed in myself because Justin believed in me. I called my mom and gushed, "I am dating *a man*! He's twenty-two, and he has facial hair!" And all we talked about was getting married and living happily ever after. The only catch?

I would need to become Catholic.

We talked about Jesus. Justin was a devout Catholic. His family was the same. Justin's Catholic Jesus was just as harsh and difficult to understand as the Jesuses I brought to the relationship, so I figured He must be legit.

We married at his tiny childhood parish, and we moved into a little blue house at the edge of his hometown. We went to Mass every Sunday with his parents and his siblings and their spouses in the pew next to us.

While Justin worked for his dad at a mechanical contracting company, he encouraged me to pursue my dream of a degree in journalism. He had always struggled with dyslexia, and he urged me to go to Abilene Christian University and see about being tested for learning disabilities. And in the fall after we were married, I was enrolled at ACU, where, with the school's programs for dyslexia, I thrived like I never had before. I graduated with honors, with our firstborn, Mary Margaret (Maggie)—yeah, we were that Catholic—in the audience.

So smitten was I with Justin and country living that I surrendered my pursuit of Jane Pauley-ism and got a degree in family and consumer sciences (yes, home ec). I made homemade yeast rolls and apple pies from scratch with flaky crusts. I went on to get a graduate degree in education, counseling, and human development. I was positive I would rewrite the face of education and show every awful principal and teacher that they messed with the wrong blonde.

I had my master's degree orals on a Wednesday and gave birth to John the next morning. Luke followed quickly after (did I mention we were excellent Catholics?). And then Sophie. Ten years after Sophie was born we opened our hearts and home to adoption and foster care, and now our brood has expanded to that once-dreaded number of seven.

When Maggie was about four, we moved from Justin's small town to Abilene, twenty minutes away, and bought a little mid-century house near one of the local universities. It was a white dollhouse, decorated with red shutters and a matching front door that I adored. There were seasonal bulbs across the front of the tiny house and a weird tree that had fuzzy pink blossoms. I likened it to a Dr. Seuss tree. The backyard looked like a park with six enormous pecan trees, a swing set, and a little picnic table. I have fond memories of those years, building our family and cooking and playing with my babies.

At that time in my life, I thought I had it all sewn up. Handsome husband, beautiful children, and a large church community for the icing on the cake. I had just finished my graduate work, and Justin was working at a successful mechanical design company. We were happy, and it was a delightful time. I thought I had complete control. Thaw a pound of ground beef, bake cookies, play with the kids in the backyard, cut the crust off their sandwiches, walk at the YMCA, dot my *i*'s and cross my *t*'s, and all would be well.

With an undergraduate degree in home economics, I prided myself on my homemaking abilities. I even spoke to a couple of MOPS meetings about Cleanliness, Godliness, and the Perfect Home. Be forewarned, esteem yourself not. There is nowhere to go but down. One evening after I had hosted a baby shower at our house, Justin went to the bathroom to get some Tylenol for a fussy toddler. When he emerged from the bathroom, he addressed Maggie, full-name irritated.

"Mary Margaret! You must flush the potty when you are finished! But more important, you must tell Mommy and Daddy when you are out of toilet paper."

Maggie looked up from her coloring book, somewhat disgusted that he had aired such a private matter so openly, and said, "I just use the little hand towel next to the sink when I am out of toilet paper."

Justin and I gasped, utterly horrified. And Maggie rolled her eyes and said, "Calm down. I put it back after I use it." I think Justin and I spent the rest of the night bleaching everything. The next day he installed paper towel dispensers in all the bathrooms.

My house was clean, or appeared to be. The fancy hand towels added to the illusion. But the cobalt-blue towel with a little orange goldfish embroidered on the front was hiding a nasty secret. And this icky metaphor applies to all sinners. Things can be beautiful on the outside and a horror show under a microscope.

I have been guilty of trying to put on a show that would be coveted by others, thereby leading them into a state of sin and despair. Piously I would dress my best and work my tail off to delude onlookers of my greatness. And I can't help but wonder... When I was doing a "fabulous" job, everything was going the way it should, did others really believe that I had it all together? That life as me was the most fun you could have? Now I pray that He would dwell in me, and I am more than willing to stay at a very low place on the totem pole. In that place, flat on my face, I am nearer the cross.

I spent the better part of the next sixteen years trying to maintain order and neatness. I taught a class on "Home as Sanctuary." I find this quite ironic now. When Real Jesus and I finally started getting tight, I learned to appreciate the messes and embrace them rather than frantically trying to bleach them. This embracing had nothing to do with me or my tidiness or my abilities. I can scream from the mountaintops that I have a master's degree, but the pedigree doesn't keep me from finding myself half naked in Walmart (don't worry, I'll get to that). And I can decorate with knick-knacks, fancy candles, and doilies, but a kid is probably going to use that doily to clean his bum. It's okay. Jesus still loves us.

I still try to maintain some level of order, and I love beautiful things. I like for the laundry to be caught up and the floors to be clean, but this isn't what makes my home respectable. Jesus is the only factor that makes this dwelling acceptable. If you are a horrible housekeeper and are crazy in love with Jesus, this is where His greatness is bred. If Jesus resides in you—no matter the type of structure (mansion, apartment, cabin, or trailer) you live in—you are on sacred ground. He makes all things clean, new, and blameless. Assuming you are willing to let go of the reins and let Him teach and convict you.

In spite of the fact that we now have seven children aged one to twenty-two, this is a slightly easier season in our lives. Financially, nope. Emotionally, no way. Without drama, HA! No. Things are much more complicated now than they were in 2001. But there is an ease in not trying to be perfect or impress my neighbors. Maybe because we have been outnumbered for so long. I am not sure. There was just a point where I had to relinquish my control. Once that happened, the blessings poured out.

Right before Sophie's arrival, we moved just outside of Abilene, to the school district I swore I would never live in, where I originally met High School Jesus. Justin built us a big ranch house on two acres. We became very involved in a large Catholic church near our home. When I say *very involved*, I mean it. We taught Sunday school, participated in every event, and attended daily Mass.

Yes, *daily*.

Every morning we proudly took our children to Mass. And when I say *proudly*, I mean that too. In what was obviously a pride issue, we went every morning at seven o'clock and participated in the thirty-minute Mass. And the elderly daily Mass-goers "oohed" and "awed" over the marvel of our dedication; our dedication to our marvelousness.

We looked fabulous.

And like the notorious cobalt-blue hand towel with an embroidered goldfish on the front—the towel Maggie used to clean her bum—appearances were deceiving. Under a microscope, we were a hot mess. We tried so hard to keep up with the Joneses we were continually strapped for cash. We worshipped and prayed in vain— for the show. We were further from Real Jesus on our knees in front of an enormous oak crucifix than ever before. When my bridled snark and smothered journalistic streak began to balk at some of the teachings, our "friends" wouldn't tolerate my arguments. They ended in humiliating confrontations where I was accused of being sacrilegious and uninformed.

Which was accurate.

How I have failed and how I have succeeded were at the core of my search for the Real Jesus. The insane and ridiculous, the less than, the more than, the trials, the burdens, and the triumphs are at the heart of the sacred and the sticky that have drawn me to this place, a place that looked very much like freedom and what I would soon call New Covenant Living.

The song and dance I continued to perform over the years was all about what I could do to *make* Jesus love me. Like a lost little girl on yet another foreign playground, in yet another new town, left out and alone, I was desperate for Him to pick me. In the midst of all of this, there was a frantic part of me that knew I needed to find the Real Jesus. But He was muddled by Mormon Jesus, Americanized Jesus, Catholic Jesus, Baptist Jesus, Mean Jesus, New Age Jesus, Hippie Jesus, and a wealth of other characters by whom I had been misled. (The quest for truth and Real Jesus is muddied further by religion, man, your grandparents' world, the new world, religiosity, tolerance, and affluence.) I wanted Jesus, and not my parents' Jesus or the Jesus from Sunday school as told by a cucumber and a tomato in a vegetarian musical. Not Tent Revival Jesus, not High School Jesus, not any of the other characters that bounced in and out of my life. I wanted Jesus with me, wandering my halls, searching my heart. Still, He evaded me.

I kept waiting for something spectacular to happen. I wanted to be free from the shackles of overwhelming fear. I wanted to overcome strongholds. I wanted to walk in the freedom the churched-up people spoke of, the freedom of salvation.

Stew on this: You can't be *kind of* saved. If you are drowning and I come by in my boat and pull you out of the water and take you to shore, you are saved. If I only throw you a life jacket, you still have to tread water. I was treading water. I was in the pew professing salvation but working to make it happen. *And nothing happened from my meager attempts to be God.*

So I faked it. And I worked harder than most, looking like I was in this deep relationship with the risen Son of God. I wore out relationships with my questions and my need. I wanted to be like the answer givers seemed to be. I did things to please these people. I helped them decorate, cooked them meals, babysat their kids, and showered them with gifts—gifts we couldn't afford. All of this in the hopes that they would share with me the secret to what I saw as a textbook walk with a perfect and unreachable God.

I had no peace about so many of their practices. Perhaps my Mormon roots and jaded spirit made me combative to law, but I would almost instinctively question any doctrine that was "cross plus." Jesus saved you on the cross...Oh, and you also need to do this and this and this to earn that salvation. The work depends on you, not Him.

Later we would make a heartbroken exodus from the Catholic Church, but on this day, overcome by my questions, I marched into the confessional on a Saturday afternoon in search of answers. The chapel was empty when I entered. I quietly knelt in the confessional and began to yammer.

"Father, why do I have to work and work? If my actions grant me some sort of favor with God, why did Jesus need to die? Why did God allow His only Son to be brutally slain? Why do my works matter? Must I really do all this? Must my children do this?"

The priest—a man whom I still love—spent forty-five minutes teaching me and explaining. Finally, I stood and thanked him and walked out of the confessional happy and confident in my new-found knowledge.

When I left the confessional, the chapel was no longer empty. Instead, it was full of immensely curious, increasingly impatient would-be confessors. Among the irritated parishioners glaring at me and muttering "Jezebel" was one of the little boys from my Sunday school class. The moment he saw me step from the confessional, he yelped, "Mrs. Amerine, what did you *do*?" And his mom popped him upside the back of his head.

I laugh now at that humiliating moment. What did I do?

Everything. I had tried everything to be saved.

The Catholic crew made the sign of the cross and kissed their fingers if we drove past a cemetery or parish. They sat in the pews next to us early every morning for daily Mass. And as we exited the church, they talked about how beautiful the Mass was. I would nod my head and agree, but I was lying. I didn't get it. And I am not saying they weren't having an amazing experience, but I wasn't. I memorized the vocabulary. I bought Catholic homeschool curriculum. I went to Sunday school and apologetics classes so I could defend what I believed I should believe. Still, unbeknownst to these peers, I lay at the foot of our son John's bed night after night terrorized with the notion he would die before his tenth birthday. I am not sure why the great tormentor created this fear, but oh my, it worked. I believed for so long that John specifically wouldn't survive his childhood because I was such a disaster. (Looking back, I suspect John's failed hearing tests and breathing treatments were the catalyst for my fears.)

No matter how hard I tried, no Bible study, Mass, rosary, tent revival, or ritual set me free of those beliefs. Still, I prayed rosaries and begged that he be spared. If I was perfect, if my efforts were grand enough, maybe God would choose to save him. I was a slave to my nightmares.

Eventually, convinced I was being punished for rebelling against the church, I drove John seventy-five miles away to walk through the Jubilee door.* I made John go through seven times. We stayed for Mass; we professed its beauty. And later that night, when I thought that I had resolved the horror, I found myself at the foot of his bed once more, praying rosary after rosary, petrified, exhausted, and without the hope of ever being free.

---

* The Jubilee door was opened by Pope John Paul II in 2000 as part of a Year of Jubilee in which Catholics could obtain an "indulgence" (remission of punishment for sins) by walking through the door, offering certain prayers, and meeting other criteria. Other Jubilee doors were opened in designated churches and shrines around the world.

This Jesus was the opposite of Real Jesus. I was afraid of Him and His wrath. He must have been a monster. He broke my heart, He wore down my spirit, and He ran me ragged with His malicious lies. I could barely keep up the façade. With a voice that cracked when I spoke, I told stories to my peers about "the beauty" of my deep Catholic walk. All the while, I was dying of thirst, starving to death, clinging to the threads of the altar décor and legalistic, ritualistic pomp and circumstance of a made-up Jesus.

Finally, one night, the rosary cutting through my flesh as I clung to it, I cried out from the floor of my son's bedroom, "Please, I can't anymore. Please. I give up! I just give up! Help me. If You are real, help me."

Looking back, perhaps that was the moment when the actual unraveling began.

7

Scare-Me-Up Jesus

I do not consider that I have made it my own. But one thing I do: forgetting what lies behind and straining for to what lies ahead, I press on toward the goal for the prize of the upward call of God in Christ Jesus.

PHILIPPIANS 3:13-14 ESV

When our oldest daughter, Maggie, was a toddler, my parents had this toy that Maggie called "the scare-me-up bunny." It was essentially a jack-in-the-box, only a bunny came out instead of a clown. She would bring it to one of us and say, "Open da scare-me-up-bunny." And then she would put her chubby toddler hands over her eyes, peeping through sticky fingers, and wait for the bunny to "scare her up."

Maggie had this angel-like habit of patting her chest over her heart when anything scared or moved her. Once, while visiting my parents who were living in South America, we saw a homeless man on the side of the road in Venezuela. Maggie's brown eyes swelled, her lip quivered, and she patted her chest. She couldn't have been more than two—still, her heart ached so much that it needed to be consoled.

I digress.

One of us would turn the crank on the toy, the music would play...then slow and then...*POP!* The scare-me-up bunny would erupt from the box, and Maggie would squeal and then pat her racing heart.

I treated Jesus that way too. I asked Him to abide by my wishes, and then I turned the crank. If He showed up and did as I asked, I was elated and shocked, and I updated my Facebook status with delight at an answered prayer. If He popped out of the box in which I kept Him with a different answer than I'd requested, I would just shove Him back in the box and kept turning the prayer crank to hear myself talk and hopefully, eventually get what I wanted the way I wanted it.

I blurred the lines between a scary Jesus and a real devil. I feared Him, expecting Him to pop up and punish me by killing someone I loved, causing us financial ruin, or making me add another twelve pounds.

Before I go any further, allow me to apologize to the widow, the breast cancer survivor, and the mamma who buried her baby. What you are about to witness is my belief that I was owed something I was not.

Around the time I turned forty-two, I got sick. We had finalized our adoption of Sam, and we had decided that he would benefit from a sibling closer to his age. We had been diligently working on our foster care license and were nearing the finish line. In the midst of that, Justin's mom entered the last stages of her battle with cancer, and we moved her into our home where she lived out the remainder of her days.

And then, without much warning, I was unable to get out of bed one morning. My limbs weighed a thousand pounds. My head pounded. My joints were on fire. I was *sick*.

I was accustomed to not feeling great. I suffer from an autoimmune disease called Hashimoto's, a thyroid condition that causes your body to destroy its own thyroid gland. The symptoms range in magnitude. Some days I am just tired; other days I have debilitating fatigue and body aches. The majority of days I struggle with weight gain (wait, that's every single blasted day). But on this day, something was really wrong.

I called Justin, and he arranged to work from home. I slept for sixteen hours. I woke up, crawled to the bathroom, crawled back to the bed, and slept twelve hours more. I only wearily opened my eyes after Justin woke me to take me to the doctor.

After a series of inconclusive tests, my dad made arrangements for me to come to Houston and be seen by a specialist. She ran the same tests and then gave me a card for an appointment with another doctor for the next morning. I was feeling somewhat better, having been on precautionary antibiotics and steroids for close to two weeks, so I drove myself to a medical building in The Woodlands, about thirty minutes from my parents' home.

The three-story clinic was hidden among enormous pine trees, and I was surprised to find I could only park valet. Odd, I thought, for a doctor's office. I pulled up to the front of the snazzy clinic and handed my keys over to the valet and made my way into the building. I was greeted by a woman who asked for my appointment referral and insurance. Then she handed me a menu and told me to choose a beverage.

I ordered a Grande Vanilla Cappuccino extra hot with one sugar packet, and she told me to be seated, that she would bring me my coffee shortly. This, folks, is the way waiting rooms should be. After a delightful twelve-minute wait, sucking down fantastic java, a chubby nurse made her way toward me.

"Mrs. Amerine?" she asked.

"Yes, that's me."

"Hello, my name is Trish. You can follow me this way."

I gathered my things, and we made pleasantries to the elevator and then to the third floor. The doors opened to an office behind perfectly clean glass. I stood motionless. I tried to adjust my eyes. The elevator walls seemed to be closing in on me. And Trish gently touched my arm and compassionately cooed, "Mrs. Amerine, this is where you will go in for your appointment."

I willed myself out of delirium.

"Y-y-yes," I stammered. "Yes, okay."

"Honey, are you all right?"

"Yes. Um. Yes, I am okay, thank you."

She patted my arm. "Go right inside there and they will prepare you for your appointment."

Still, I stood. The elevator door shut. Sensing I was alone, I read the bewildering words on the door before me out loud.

"Premier Liver Cancer Specialists."

I said it twice. At this point, all I was certain of was no one had said anything about liver cancer.

I was offered another cappuccino, but since I couldn't swallow I declined. Soon, alone in a hospital gown, seated on a paper sheet, I googled *liver cancer*, and then tried not to cry as I recognized symptom after symptom that the illness and I had in common. I started a text to my mom: "THIS IS A LIVER CANCER SPECIALIST!? They have valet parking and gourmet coffee."

I deleted it.

I started to text Justin, but what would I say? "Hey, babe, how much am I insured for? Don't forget to feed the dogs."

I deleted that text too.

Finally, after an eternity, the doctor came in to tell me that I didn't have liver cancer, but I was, in fact, "fat and forty." And that most people in my condition felt like crap. That will be $700.

And while I may very well have been "fat and forty," she was wrong about one thing. I was very ill. Upon my return home I got progressively worse. My mom suggested I see a chiropractor. At the appointment, as I poured out my complaints, he inquired, "Does your mouth or jaw hurt?"

"Yes, my jaw. Why?"

Nine days later I lay in a hospital bed overlooking, well, nothing. (This is West Texas, y'all. Not a lot of scenery.) I was finally on the mend after a tooth extraction—a cure to the silent abscess that had been slowly killing me. All the pain, all the drama and lethargy, all the awfulness had been due to the one thing I hadn't been loyal to: *flossing*. A bad tooth, seriously?

It would be another two weeks before I was well enough to drive. And when that day came, I got ready to go to the grocery store, entirely confident things were back to normal.

My normal shouldn't really be a standard by which we gauge things. Bloated from IV fluids, steroids, high-potency antibiotics, and limited movement, I was irritated to discover that none of my clothes fit. I finally found a black-and-white tie-dyed full-length Bohemian skirt at the back of my closet. The stretchy material was actually quite comfy, which was all I really cared about at this point. At least I was getting out of the house.

I drove through Starbucks and grabbed some coffee before heading to the store. I was kid-free and acting like a sixteen-year-old on the first day with her license, although I was going grocery shopping and not to the mall with Daddy's credit card. I grabbed a shopping cart and began to fill my basket with delicious and nutritious items. This was a new day. We were going to put this season behind us.

As I pushed my basket through Walmart, I meticulously crossed off each item on my list and then…I tripped over something. I looked down and to my profound shock saw my skirt entwined in the shopping cart wheel. It was completely off my body.

When I say completely off my body, I mean the only thing that kept the skirt associated to me was one of my flip-flopped feet that was still in the waistband on the floor. The rest of the skirt was tightly twisted into a ball around the basket's wheel.

There I stood, in a T-shirt and my Hanes Her Way yellow cotton briefs. I couldn't bend over. I couldn't look behind me or in front of me. I was half naked in Walmart. The stuff nightmares are made of was now my full reality. I casually squatted to try and untangle my skirt. I heard a burst of laughter and then what sounded like an iPhone camera click. I tugged and pulled. I could not get the skirt undone. I stood up and braced one foot on the basket and pulled as hard as I could. The material ripped, the basket bucked, and my coffee went flying into the air and exploded onto my white T-shirt. With the skirt mangled and torn, I slipped it back on, grabbed my purse, and ran. (To this day, I haven't been back to that Walmart. Every once in a while those "worst Walmart photos" articles float around on Facebook, and I click through, fully prepared to have made the list—me and my bum. Nothing yet.)

I made it to my car and came unglued. There in my Buick I threw the mother of all fits.

I broke up with Jesus.

Fury rose from I don't know where, but I unleashed a vulgar assault on the Savior of the World, the likes of which should have resulted in a lightning storm, complete with flying livestock and softball-sized hail. Every unanswered prayer, every lost hope, every medical bill, unsold property, car repair, illness, and miscellaneous instance that I could blame on Jesus, I did. When I was finished, I committed to yoga and a lacto/ovo/vegetarian lifestyle (so I could still have cheese omelets and ice cream).

I started my car and plugged in my iPhone and selected the song "Say Something" by indie pop duo A Great Big World. And I belted that song at the top of my weary lungs, directly to Jesus. "Say something, I'm giving up on yooooooooou." Dogs howled as I drove by. It was altogether cathartic and pathetic. I am not sure what made me believe I deserved anything better than liver cancer and Walmart nudity, but I was certain I was done chasing after a god who wouldn't treat me better.

The travesty didn't quite end there. Jesus was a habit. And He was a hard habit to break. *Oh well,* I decided. *I will break the habit, be in control of my own destiny, and finally move past the fallacy that there is a higher power looking out for me.*

I loved the rebellious freedom of not messing with Jesus. I had done good things. I had homeschooled, adopted, fostered, eaten organic carrots, and nursed my dying mother-in-law to the other side. Still, Scare-Me-Up Jesus had me lose months to a ridiculous illness that turned out, in the end, to be just a bad tooth. I could do all that nonsense on my own without being shackled to a would-be Messiah who didn't seem to ever listen to me and was impossible to please.

I couldn't bring myself to take Stolen Jesus down from the mantel. So I just didn't go in the formal living room, like, ever. And then, just as I felt I had hit my stride, tragedy struck.

You may have heard the story on the news yourself. Kent Brantly, son-in-law of one of my closest friends, Lisa, is a medical missionary who was working in Liberia with Samaritan's Purse. While treating Ebola patients, he contracted the disease himself.

The days that followed the news were a roller coaster of hopes that were dashed, reignited, and dashed again. We watched in horror as this family we love teetered on the brink of losing Kent—doctor, husband, father, son, and servant to the least of these.

On Friday, August 1, 2014, I drove about town in a fog, my hymn "Say Something" blaring on my stereo. At the time I didn't know that the next day Kent Brantly would be safely back on U.S. soil, the first United States citizen to return to our country and survive Ebola. Angry and emotionally spent, I was at a stoplight when I saw the sign: Mission Water Slide. A gaggle of tweens held signs, and one ran up to my car. Exhausted from the emotion of Kent's continued demise, I stared blankly at the perky girl who explained they would wash my car for a donation for their church youth trip to Splash Mountain. I murmured, "What is the mission?" and she chirped, "We are passing out brown bag lunches to the homeless, and then we are going to Splash Mountain to celebrate." I wanted to ask, "Celebrate what?" But a car horn blared behind me.

I didn't contribute.

That night my husband and I sat on the porch and stared at the stars and wept. At that point we knew that Kent had barely made it through the night.

Mission Water Slide flashed in my mind.

Who is this Jesus who funds trips to water parks with a payment of a ham sandwich to a homeless guy, and destroys a doctor who laid down his life for the least of these? I refused to pretend I was wrestling with this Jesus anymore. He made no sense. There was no pleasing or appeasing Him. I went to bed and let the tears soak my pillow. The last thing I remember was Justin's voice, "Our Father, who art in heaven..."

Months later, having already paid to travel to a Christian writer's conference, I attended with a chip on my shoulder and a hypocritical manuscript in my bag. One evening, unable to stomach another session on how much I was loved by Jesus and how important my writing was to kingdom glory, I wandered into the refreshment area.

It was there I met a woman named Katrina, a teacher and former missionary in Papua New Guinea. As we giggled with our friends and voiced our weary opinions about the world, the future, and religion, I spouted off, "I broke up with Jesus."

And that is when Katrina said, straight-faced and shamelessly, "It's easy to break up with Americanized Jesus. It's impossible to break up with the Real Jesus."

All of the Jesuses began to come together in that moment. The lies were mine to sort through, but the truth was right before me. I broke up with Jesus because I didn't get my way. As if He could be manipulated into doing what I wanted when I wanted Him to. As if He owed me more than He had already paid. If I thought I was humiliated to be naked in Walmart, it was nothing compared to the shame I felt when, not too many days later, I made my way to the formal living room and bowed before Him in my prayer chair.

On my knees that night in front of Stolen Jesus, I couldn't even speak. My mind was a clatter as I rehashed what was obvious to Him. And even in the midst of my breakdown, He waited. Perhaps my heart and my head weren't prepared to fully know Him when I was baptized and saved in Victoria, Texas, all those years ago, but I had asked Him into my heart, and I believe He had stayed. It was a one-way ticket. He stayed.

Somewhere in the fog of what I had created Him to be, the Real Jesus's character was busting through the lies and making a grand entrance in my life.

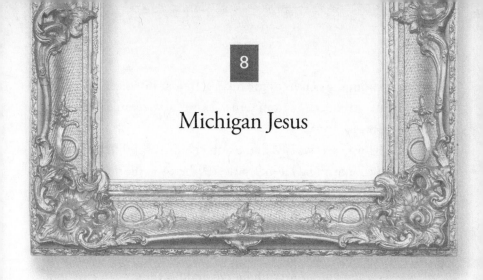

8

Michigan Jesus

*Ask and it will be given to you; seek
and you will find; knock and the
door will be opened to you.*

MATTHEW 7:7

Where was I to begin? How do you undo forty-some years of misunderstandings and counterfeit beliefs and overlooking Real Jesus? I knew I had been set free from the trap of believing Jesus was some kind of lucky amulet, I believed He was real, and I knew I did not truly know Him. But if I were justly saved, why was I so unhappy? Why didn't I have the solutions? Why wasn't I perfected by the blood of the Lamb, like everyone else *seemed* to be? To my core I wanted Him to be real, and I wanted Him to actually save me.

I have been baptized four times. I have been dunked in a tub behind the pulpit at an Assembly of God, sprinkled by the Lutherans, poured over by the Catholics, and once, all alone in a lake, I begged Him to make that time stick, to set me free in the name of the Father, the Son, and the Holy Spirit...or please just don't let me come up from the depths of my misery. In that instance, I gained only a nasty ear infection from some Texas lake water microbe that nested in my ear canal.

Still, I saw others washed in the water and emerge different, better. So why not me? Did He like me less? Where was the mystic? The gift of tongues? The transcendent holy moments that evaded me? No, I had no business fishing for men or professing the kingdom of heaven. Not to my kids, not to my neighbor, not to anyone.

After that night in my prayer chair before Stolen Jesus, I had torn down the false gods of my childhood, and now it was time to go in search of the Real Jesus. The hard work of uncovering lies about Jesus left me at ground zero. I knew who He wasn't. Now I needed to fill in the gaps of who He was.

Inviting Him to reveal His true self had left me plagued with denial, tears, acceptance, more tears, a few nasty tantrums, and the welcomed release that comes from forgiveness that He alone manifests.

The person most challenging me to dig deeper into my pursuit of Jesus was my best friend, Kim. And she wasn't verbally pressuring me—I just admired how she got where she was going. Whether either of us knew it or not, she started me on this path to the discovery of Real Jesus ages ago.

"She's kind of scary, Justin..."

My husband was only half listening to me. "Scary how?" he asked.

I began to expound. "She says whatever is in her head, like, without caring if it is going to offend anyone."

Justin looked up from cutting tomatoes. "She sounds fantastic." And she is.

I met Kim at our children's preschool in 1998. Her oldest, Joe, and my oldest, Maggie, were in class together, and we were both lugging car seats with infants along with our preschoolers' backpacks. I walked into the classroom one day to find Kim "speaking her mind," which I never did, and I quickly ran to my car. I despise confrontation, probably because I am bad at it. Chalk it up to her Michigan roots—Kim will say anything. I have never been to Michigan, but if this is where she gets it, I cannot go there.

So I sidestepped Kim. My gift of hospitality was far outweighed by my inability to handle her forthrightness. She seemed like she wanted to chat, and although she is a tiny thing, I was intimidated by her.

One afternoon, about two forty-five, I wandered into the library, lugging a diaper bag, a ginormous baby John, and Maggie walking behind me. I collapsed down at a tiny table with tiny chairs. She was at the tiny table next to ours, and I was too loaded down to escape.

"Oh, hi, Kim. What are y'all doing?" Maggie and her son flopped onto the floor next to each other and began looking at books.

"Killing the day," Kim said. "I hate the stretch after naptime before Mark gets home."

I gasped, "Me too! I can hardly stand it. They are the longest hours of the day. I try and get out and do something so I don't cry and eat Cheetos all afternoon!"

She invited me to her house the next day for the two-forty-five stretch. And so began our friendship.

When I arrived at her home, she opened the door to the cleanest and most well-organized house I had ever seen; to this day I have not seen its match. If you want to feel bad about your housekeeping abilities, go to Kim's. She has a little drawer next to the back door that has a Sharpie, Ziploc bags, and tape in it. I wondered why, and then one day I said, "I just need to label Maggie's snack before we go on the field trip," and she opened that drawer. I covet that drawer. I tried to have one of those drawers once. It didn't work out.

So this is her reception as I walk in the door of her picturesque home: "I do not believe in God. I know you are from around here, and everyone around here believes in God. If you are going to try and *save me*, I am not interested."

Fair enough. Kim was in luck: I am not only not confrontational, but I also am not pushy. We sat on the deck, drank iced tea, and watched the kids play. We laughed, talked, and got to know each other, and from then on we were basically inseparable.

I am as tall as she is short, as blonde as she is brunette, as Scottish-Norwegian as she is Assyrian, as passive as she is aggressive, and as religious as she is...well, that's the thing. Kim can spot a Pharisee from twenty feet, and she will call you on it. And at first, it's awkward. I am not used to this behavior at all. But I cannot get enough of her. Seriously, I think she is just saying what anyone with common sense is thinking.

We are soul mates. They say opposites attract, and Kim and I not only make it scientific law, but also officially write it in stone. But our shared core? A complete lack of compassion or understanding for anyone breaking our stomach flu rules.

I kid you not, at one mommy gathering, the hostess flippantly mentioned, "Sorry I'm such a mess. The kids and I were up all night with some weird bug vomiting, and we still have a little fever, but I'm sure it's fine."

Kim jumped her one-hundred-pound, five-foot-two frame in front of the children and me; it was a black-belt karate move, arms spread wide, half squat, ready to take down this hostess if she took one step closer. She started barking, "Stay back! Jami, take the children and back away slowly. You, woman, take ten steps back from my people...When I say, go, Jami, run!" And we ran as if it were a burning building.

As we bolted to safety, we yelled warnings to innocent partygoers, "Don't go in! They're vomiting!" No one would heed our warning. They glared at us as if we were the crazy ones. One by one they wandered into the house of horrors; bless them, they couldn't be stopped.

In addition to our shared vomiting neurosis, Kim and I both have a genuine fear of flying, so no matter how long we go without seeing each other, if she is flying somewhere, I can fully expect a phone call letting me know she is leaving and reminding me that if she dies in a fiery crash to go by the house twice a week, open the blinds, and make sure the kids and Mark aren't just eating Pop Tarts and spaghetti noodles with ketchup. I think this is in her will too, but she likes the verbal comfort of saying it directly to me. We've got each other's back.

In year three of our relationship, we signed the kids up for gymnastics, which was just another way to kill time until our husbands got home. We were in a room with other mommies. And in this area was a mom with a baby in a full body cast. Everyone was hovering about, and the mom of the injured boy said, "Well, we were staying in this hotel, down in Houston, and little Dustin crawled out onto the balcony and slipped through the bars and fell four stories. And now we tell him, he must be *really* special to God because God saved his life."

Kim's back tightened, her quizzical eyebrow went up, she folded her arms (and my stomach lurched because, oh my—here we go), and she said, "Wow, God must have hated my baby, because he fell four stories and died."

I can't remember what happened after that because I think I blacked out. Seriously, when we left, me with the full intention of never going back, I was without words for half the drive home. Finally, I sputtered out, "Kim? What in the world?"

And you can believe, she told me. "How can you even stomach that? People's babies die all the time. *This God of yours has favorites?* I am not interested in that kind of God at all. When we had lived here less than two weeks, the church ladies came to my door, and I told them I wasn't sure I believed in God, and they said that I would go straight to hell. *I was holding Joey,* and they told me I was going to *hell.* I don't understand how this is a good promotion for salvation. I don't believe in God. Well, you're going to hell, and I hope your baby doesn't fall off a balcony, or you're screwed!"

I cannot think of a scenario where I would tell a mom she was going to hell, and I spend an inordinate amount of time at the Child Protective Services Agency. As followers of Jesus Christ, we are to share and display the *Good* News. That is precisely what He said when He sent out His disciples. He literally told them, "Go into all the world and preach the *Good News* to everyone" (Mark 16:15 NLT, emphasis added).

Kim was right. Do I want my kids to love me only because they want something from me? Or so I won't punish them? An actual relationship with Jesus shouldn't be based on peril. And I was so sorry that Jesus had been so falsely represented to her, but I am certain I believed the same thing. The only rational response was, "I'm sorry." And I was. On behalf of every Bible-belt Christian who led her to believe in this counterfeit Jesus, I was truly sorry for our awfulness.

Still, it was in that confused state that I first realized that Wrathful Jesus was exactly who I believed in. An angry god, one whom I was trying desperately to please. It would be fourteen years before he would completely unravel. Looking back, I am most grateful I didn't try and help Kim in her journey. I wasn't the one to teach her something—she really needed nothing from me but to be her friend. My relationship with Kim was the first in my life that was without religious pretense or mission. I wasn't there to save her or give her truth. I didn't confess to her that I walked to the front of any church in any town, at every pulpit call, desperate for a numinous moment where I would finally be saved...be made whole and no longer a train wreck.

We laughed, stressed, avoided stomach bugs, and brought each other heads of cabbage to reduce engorgement when our breast milk came in. And then she sought after God in a way that challenged her and exposed Him. She came to know Him. And her knowledge further proved to me that *I did not know my God.*

Jesus-speak poured from my lips, yet I knew not what I said. I thank God Kim shut me up at her doorstep. Had she not, would I have ruined a beautiful friendship by professing the ridiculousness that I believed about Jesus then? Worse still, would I have become another Christian who slighted her, misled her, and alienated her from the Lord of her heart? I shudder to think.

The great thing about Kim is that she never takes her curiosities lying down. The longer she was in the Evangelical State of Texas, the more answers she required, and so she signed up for an Episcopalian Bible course that took three years to complete.

When she finished the Old Testament, she called me and said, "Well, I think I believe all that, so I guess I am Jewish." And then when she finished the New Testament, she was pretty well convinced about that too. She wasn't mystically transformed via Door-to-Door Jesus or Pulpit-Call Jesus. And I am not necessarily criticizing those methods, but Kim wanted the whole package. She needed all the answers she could get before she said, "Yes, Lord."

He was real to her. You can't be a grand thinker like Kim and not crave relevance. God promises to reveal Himself. And Kim held

Him to it. Maybe this is where I failed in my quest. I never let Him reveal Himself. Instead of letting Him be God, I was trying to create Him into the image I saw fit, a God who made sense. Although Kim is a critical thinker, I propose she is a deeper believer simply because she allowed Him to prove Himself through His Word.

An Ongoing Process

From the very start, even before she knew Him herself, Kim was challenging me to get to know the Real Jesus. After I blubbered through the embarrassment of breaking up with Jesus and the long night I'd spent beginning the process of dismantling all the false Jesuses, I started really reading the Gospels and praying Jesus would reveal Himself to me. I noticed that He never once said, "Please go door-to-door and threaten young mothers from the Great Lakes region with eternal damnation. Scare them to death so that they too will follow Me." He just wasn't like this. He was a gentleman. He was compassionate. He was forgiving. And while it is true, there are consequences for your life and your choices, second in my discovery was that *Jesus is not a bully.* Aside from that, I will try not to define Him for you. But know this, He is kind.

I imagine Kim's Jesus does things Michigan style. Not that He changes from one child to the next, but simply that He knows her, and He is exactly who she needs when she needs Him. And I would not have known this without knowing her and watching her fall in love with Him. I recognize now that coming to know Christ is an ongoing process. Knowing Him doesn't make the pizza sauce stain on the carpet go away (the stains at my house—Kim never has stains), but it makes the stains, bumps, bruises, and general hiccups bearable.

I never profess I have my husband entirely figured out. I never stop investing in our bond, our time together. I never stop wanting to learn more about him. Why should it be any different in my relationship with Jesus?

In my quest, I had a sincere desire to stay in a fetal position at the foot of the cross. I was broken, but I was saved. I knew He would lead me if I let Him, and there's the challenge. I do have to seek Him and pursue His wisdom. He won't bang on my door and threaten me. But He will wait outside, or behind a filing cabinet at the YMCA, and wait for me to invite Him. Once inside, everything changes—however, not in the way I first believed.

Failure Is an Option

The first step was to simply succumb to my broken state. I was and am a wreck. Admitting this was both liberating and humiliating. I knew I wanted to change, but the profound epiphany was that I didn't have to.

I am not some spiritual wizard, but Jesus showed me something about Himself when He introduced me to Kim.

She's a size 4. She follows recipes to the letter. She is beautiful, married to a handsome doctor, and you could eat off her garage floor—it's way cleaner than my kitchen. I coveted her perfection—but she was a mess. She was trying to get by, failing in ways opposite of me, and none of it had anything to do with Jesus. She denied Him and struggled...welcomed Him, and the struggles were still real. This is paramount.

At our house, we say, "Failure is an option." Failure is a place where we learn. Failure is a place where we cry out from our brokenness and experience Real Jesus. Embracing failure, admitting confusion, is the opposite of everything you might have known. But it is a utopia, where you see with fresh eyes as your mind is renewed. A confused space where you question how you got where you are and where you have been. Failure is an option, and confusion is a blessing.

If I never fail, I will never seek improvement. If I am never confused, I will not find clarity. If I am never lost, I need not be found. If I am not hungry, I do not need to be fed. If I do not grieve, then I cannot be comforted.

And perhaps that is the hardest part of this journey, admitting failure and embracing the emotions that follow closely behind. In the back of my mind, I knew I had lived my "faith" in various stages between "lukewarm" and "Texas Chainsaw Massacre." The flippancy by which I attributed failure to my Weight Watchers debacles seemed minimal compared to failing to understand the Savior I had verbally gushed over for the better part of forty years. So, after the dismantling of all the false Jesuses that night in the living room, I needed to grieve.

And I wanted to grieve this. I wanted to grieve the time I had missed out on Him, the Real Him.

I had to face the wasted time. The time I had professed a love of Jesus and been terrified of His crazy yet imaginary wrath. I was laid out, partially relieved and partly grief stricken. Getting to know Him hurt, and unearthing old injuries cut.

At the feet of Jesus, there is an abundance of wisdom about who He really is. The complexities never stop surprising me. But the simplicity I was unearthing was too good to be true and I had questions:

Why did He cry when Lazarus died? Knowing He could and would bring Him back to life, why was He sad?

How could He be hungry and not succumb to temptation but still identify with us?

Why did He pick Judas?

And what about the parable of the talents (Matthew 25:14-30)? Basically, He applauded the act of investing your money, and then later He told the rich man to sell all of his things.

The last shall be first?

The first shall be last?

Cut out your eye, do not hate, cut off your hand? These were the words that most confused me. One moment He was burying me under the law, the next He proclaimed I was free from it. Like Kim, I was full of questions. And she taught me that those questions were okay.

And I went to look for the answers in the place God promised He would be, the place He promised to reveal Himself: Scripture. But not in the way I had in the past. For the first time, I would start from the beginning of the story and work my way through. And just like it was for Kim, things would never be the same.

9

Idol Jesus

*Therefore there is now no condemnation
for those who are in Christ Jesus. For the
law of the Spirit of life in Christ Jesus has
set you free from the law of sin and death.*

ROMANS 8:1-2 NASB

I started spending a lot of evenings in my prayer chair. Just me and Stolen Jesus, talking about what was real, talking about what was false. And one evening, as I sat and pondered my past, I wrote in my journal: "Now what?" And the song "Bye-Bye-Bye" by *NSYNC popped in my head. (I promise this will make a little more sense in a minute.) Before I could go any further in discovering the Real Jesus, I had to deal with Idol Jesus.

Most of us remember the golden calves that we were warned of, but an idol can be anything that distracts us from the truth about the God of the universe. There are obvious idols, like my cell phone that keeps my focus off Jesus. And then there are the less obvious, like when we worshipped our church and its congregation more than we worshipped the God of Israel—which is just embarrassing.

And I came to terms with the truth that I had even created an Idol Jesus.

Idol Jesus is a mystical beast of a god. I worshipped at Him rather than in Him. My efforts? To appease His wrath and placate His disgust. He was a statue on an altar where I continued to offer halfhearted gifts as if they were enough. *I won't eat this cake because Jesus.* As if a bite of my sacrificial dessert is more effective or can even remotely compare to the work of the cross. I was certainly missing out (a lot of wasted cake).

My list of idols doesn't stop with the religious. Within the last seven years since I received my iPhone, the bungled mess that is my brain has become infinitely worse. I love my iPhone. It is an idol in my life. I don't know what I did with all my time before I became a slave to it. With all of its evils, it has a blessing to match. I never have to think. I never have to search. I never get lost. And I can know what my second cousin's stepsister's kids in Iowa are up to minute by minute.

Is this good? Probably not. Often, a pared-down existence in a grass hut seems like it might suit me better. (Actually, we looked into it. Well, kind of. What we investigated was a tad more luxurious: a Caribbean mini-village that was for sale. It was easy to talk ourselves into it and much easier to talk ourselves out of it. First, no electricity. Second, no running water.)

But in spite of the obvious drawbacks, I can't keep myself from longing for a simpler life. When I am not obsessively gawking at my cell phone, my mind wanders to the pictures of the mini-village on that website. The multicolored stucco cabanas, the lovely tiled steps winding gracefully in between the homes. The palm trees blowing in the sunny wind. *I wonder who I would be if all there was to distract me was the weather?* Adopt a few more babies, pack a few swimsuits, and leave it all behind. Fish, clam, eat coconuts, and focus on Jesus. It seems like it would be so much easier.

Alas, a big traditional two-story saltbox is my home. Americanized living is my cross to bear. Scoff at me all you wish. Toss this book across the room, and call me crazy. But I don't think I'm the only one who feels that a life full of affluence, social media, and constant contact is a cross to bear.

Mommy life can become an idol that Satan will gladly help me justify. Laundry, grocery shopping, my husband, my kids, a diet (or lack thereof), exercise, or a Bible study...all of it is important, but if it doesn't manifest the fruit of the Spirit and kindle a fire in my relationship with Jesus, it is an idol that robs me of Real Jesus.

My phone is one of the greatest idols of all.

iWorship

Seemingly intelligent humans are so distracted by the persistent checking of a screen it's mind boggling. We are killing each other with our cars, humiliating ourselves with our folly, and are too distracted by our phones to thank the Maker of heaven and earth for all the good He bestows upon us. It's embarrassing to be giving this lecture because I am talking about myself.

No, I haven't killed anyone by driving and texting. But I have humiliated myself and others. The first year we were transitioning our family from homeschooling into private school I took a job at a little classical school to help with tuition. All of my children were enrolled there. I was teaching kindergarten and first grade, and one of my students, Hannah, was struggling with math.

My class and the preschool class were at recess when Hannah's dad texted me. "Mrs. Amerine, can we set up a conference time?"

About the same time, I got a text from my husband. He said, "Hey, want to grab lunch?"

I sent a quick "Yes" as one response. And then I sent this: "Sure thing, baby! I don't have much time. Meet me at the deli on South

14th. Order for me. I want a turkey club, lightly toasted, no mayo, and a Diet Coke. Don't sit next to the door because I have on that short skirt you love, and it's cold out. Can't wait!"

A few moments later I got this response:

"I am not comfortable meeting you alone for lunch without my wife."

I still get physically tied in knots when I think about this.

I am too easily distracted. Truly, I should be medicated or ground myself from my phone. And actually, several months ago, I did just that.

It started at a basketball game. I was hanging out with a little foster baby on my hip. Someone across the court took a picture of me and posted it on Facebook with the caption, "We need more foster mommas like Jami Amerine."

I got in trouble. You cannot put pictures of foster children on social media. Granted, it wasn't done maliciously, it wasn't my fault, and the photographer was unfamiliar with the rule, but this lapse endangered the safety of the baby. It exposed my family and me. And it was an infringement on the child's privacy and that of her birth family.

And...

Why?

For what benefit?

I was humiliated and horrified by the exposure of the baby on Facebook. Getting your foster license is hard. We didn't do it for kicks; we did it to answer a calling on our lives. Wouldn't it be a shame if all that work—work we did with the intent to help suffering children—had been wiped out because of Facebook?

I absolutely had to reevaluate, so I put down my phone for a season. It stunk for a couple of days. And then I started writing. And writing. And writing. Letters to God, prayers, stories, and future posts. I was determined that when I picked my phone back up, I would be intentional in my use. I would no longer let it monopolize my time and energy. However, I am easily distracted by shiny things, and I continue to struggle with this commitment.

A quick digression: Feeling inadequate is my specialty. I am not a leader; I am a follower. And I am the worst kind of follower because I am desperate. I am desperate to be accepted and desperate to be a part of the crowd. If you are a leader, you can count on me to follow. The question, "If your friends all jumped off a bridge, would you?" is not an applicable threat to me. The answer is a resounding *yes!* If I had friends, I would totally jump off a bridge just because they did. When it comes to me, I follow and do what everyone else is doing so that I might fit in. I crave their validation.

I could blame Satan, or Steve Jobs, or Apple for my obsession, but the truth is I embrace it. Sure, these days, if you want to get a book published you must first have a platform, and the only way to do that is to build one via social media. But that just gives me more excuses to look at my phone. Who liked that post? How many liked that post? What time did they like that post? In what country did they like that post?

Distracted.

Repeatedly distracted. As an aspiring author, I told myself that I am justifiably distracted. It is my job to be on my phone. But at the root of my phone worship is my desire to be liked. Fifth-Grade Jesus and High School Jesus lie in wait for me to see who "likes" me. Now people can literally click a "Like" button to affirm their feelings for me. Seriously, this is fantastic to someone who spent their entire existence waiting to be liked, wanting to be popular, needing companionship. I am embarrassed to admit the depths of what it means to me to get a "Like."

An earthly "Like."

And honestly, this does my soul no good. My flesh—yes. But my heart is still parched. Still desperate. Still wandering the desert chasing golden calves.

iHeart #boybands

Isn't Satan talented? How quickly we fall prey to the diabolical lie that someone or something will satisfy our hearts. Idol worship is being obsessed with anything that takes the focus off of God.

Confession time: I *love* boy bands. I have been accused of marrying Justin so I could keep my collection of "I love Justin," as in *Justin Timberlake*, memorabilia. (I plead the fifth.) Boyz II Men, New Edition, Backstreet Boys, *NSYNC, One Direction, the Jonas Brothers—I just love that type of high-pitched harmony. I won't even bother to apologize.

A few years ago, on an anniversary trip, Justin (Amerine) and I were checking into a hotel, and the staff was just abuzz with excitement. The girl checking us in said, "*NSYNC just checked out of the hotel! They met here in Dallas to hang out and catch up like the old days! We got Justin Timberlake's autograph! We're keeping their towels! The manager said we could! Do you want one?" Since I was checking into a hotel for a romantic weekend with my hubby, I thought it best to say no, but *I really wanted one of those used towels*!

Recently, Justin Timberlake was coming to Houston, and my brother bought his wife and me tickets. I was beyond jazzed. I had heard that Timberlake was a legendary performer and that it would be a show I would not soon forget.

And it was great. Kelly and I sang along to all the songs, the dancing was amazing, and the whole production was, as promised, incredibly impressive. It was a first-rate concert, and I loved it.

I had to sneak out during one set to find a restroom, and in the bathroom were two women about my age, forty-something. They were consoling each other, and were both dreadfully upset and crying. From the stall I was able to figure out that they were upset because their backstage passes were not valid for this concert and they were shattered. One of the women was heaving-crying and lamenting, "I love him so much. How can this happen? I must see him." To which the other one said, "I know. This is the saddest day of my life. But we'll catch up with him in Dallas."

I couldn't contain my giggles. It was like a *Saturday Night Live* sketch. Were they serious?

As much as I wanted to watch their drama, I couldn't stay. I wanted to watch the concert more than I wanted to watch this lunacy in the women's bathroom. However, the encounter with these Timberlake fangirls stayed on my mind for a while. They actually remind me of another duo I saw in Dallas.

It was my daughter Sophie's eighth birthday, and we were out celebrating with my sister, sister-in-law, and nieces. One of our birthday meals was at The Bistro inside the American Girl Doll Store, a reservation-only café that serves overpriced macaroni and cheese and star-shaped sandwiches to girls *and their dolls*. We sat down with the girls, arranged the girls' dolls into their high chairs, and began looking over our menus.

My sister nudged me, and I looked up to see two women being seated at the table next to us. They were both in their late fifties, dressed alike...and *dressed like their dolls*. Yep, they had dolls. They were caring for their dolls as if they were alive. We could not help but stare. They even pretended to feed their dolls, and went so far as to ask the dolls questions about their day. After our lunch, we exited the bistro at the same time as these women. They had elaborate baby carriages for their dolls and proceeded to the hair salon counter to get the dolls' hair styled.

We couldn't stop watching. Later, when they picked up their

dolls at the salon, one of them began to cry about how "beautiful" her doll looked. They took pictures, and before we left, we made sure we heard them checking out at a register for a grand total of $776. As they departed, a clerk called after them, "See you fun girls next Saturday!" to which one replied, "Oh, you know it!"

Now, I will stop here to interject, I do not know the Timberlake groupies or the American Doll ladies' hearts, and I promise I'm not standing piously in judgment (I will show my bare heinie again shortly; be patient). I have things I obsess over too. But these stories remind me that I don't want to continue to make mistakes that separate me from the joy of being obsessed with Real Jesus. The gauntlet of obsessions can't even be listed in order of most harmless to most harmful. Anything can become an idol if it shadows our relationship with Jesus, making *all idols most dangerous.*

Church Idol

I am more convinced than ever that the Catholic Church was an idol in our lives—and not the Jesus part of the church. Our church had become a space that was so social and political, it dominated our lives in a way that had nothing to do with Jesus Christ. When we finally left, we felt like we had lost our identity. Surely leaving meant that we were separating from Jesus Himself. But once we stepped back, we realized we were very wrong.

And it's not just Catholics. Idol worship takes place in Protestant churches too. We worship the talented music director or pastor; we worship the Sunday school teachers and the décor. Our Americanized religion goes so far as to say, "You should come to my church if you want the Holy Spirit. The Church of the Fountain of Truth out by the mall has valet parking and a coffee bar, and Pastor is so close to God I just cry and cry every Sunday."

Now, your pew may be the very place God meets you and it all comes together in a symphony of prophecy and ecstasy. The key is the relationship. Are you enthralled by Jesus Christ or the cute new minister and his perfect wife and kids? The apostle Paul told us in Hebrews 10:25 not to neglect the assembly—this is where we would be encouraged and held accountable for the truth. But the assembly cannot be the answer. If your pastor cheats on his perfect wife, your faith shouldn't be shaken. If the new youth wing burns down and half the congregation goes south and the other half meets in the youth minister's garage, you and Jesus should still be all good. Furthermore, we must also remember Peter encourages us: "His divine power has given us everything we need for a godly life through our knowledge of him who called us by his own glory and goodness" (2 Peter 1:3).

Everything. So in seasons where the pew is shaken—say during a move to a new town or a church scandal—He alone is not just *enough,* He is *everything.* With man there is always folly. Always, every time a man lets us down, Jesus never fails. So while we shouldn't neglect meeting as a body of believers, we find in 1 John 2:27, "The anointing you received from him remains in you, and you do not need anyone to teach you. But as his anointing teaches you about all things and as that anointing is real, not counterfeit— just as it has taught you, remain in him."

We have a precise formula for Americanized church. This is good, but it doesn't make me good. Friend and teacher Tricia Gunn says it most eloquently: "The Law is good and holy, but it doesn't make me good and holy."[1] So while *Sunday school, praise and worship, sermon, potluck, life group, choir practice, Wednesday-night Scripture study, repeat* is good for you, it doesn't add to or subtract from the work of the cross.

The litmus test for an idol is what your life looks like without it. Me without my phone is pathetic. It is my favorite possession. I can ask it how to make clam chowder or how to get a grease stain off my shirt and it knows. It alerts me to people actively liking me. It lets me know what I need from the store, where my kids are, and what time the worship service begins.

All these things seem good, until they become more important than asking Jesus to show me something significant. Something I might have missed as I stared at that marvelous screen.

Counterfeit Christs

I was recently waiting for a foster child at CPS, and a tiny newborn baby girl was brought into the office. She was being removed from her parents. I use the term *parents* loosely. The entire scenario reeked of dysfunction. I was in the far corner of the room, and they were spread out in the hall blocking the door. I was trapped in the chamber watching the horror that was occurring. I stayed in my chair and tried to pretend I was reading a magazine. What unfolded was a slew of vulgarity from the birth father, the likes of which I have never heard. The verbal abuse toward the mother and the caseworkers was relentless. Finally, the caseworker threatened to call the police, and the parents sat down and listened to their instructions. They were to be "clean" at the next drug test, they were to check in with their probation officers, they were to prepare their apartment according to the instructions on the paper the caseworker provided them, and they were to find a new home for their dog. I looked up just as the caseworker said this and realized the baby had been severely injured, obviously by the dog.

The parents begin to scream and holler again. This time the mother yelled, "YOU AIN'T TAKING MY DAWG, YOU BEEP-ITY BEEP BEEP BEEP! That dawg is my life!" (Make sure to read that with a Texas twang.) Long story short, the police were called, a foster family came for the baby, and then animal control showed up to get paperwork from the social worker and take pictures of the baby. That's when the real drama started; the parents and a grandmother were arrested because of this dog, which had so obviously hurt their *child*.

Now, I assume you think I am going to accuse these people of idol worship of their beloved Rottweiler, and while I probably could, the idol worship actually fell to me. I was so shaken by this display of callousness and ignorance I could not stop quaking. Once my foster child was finished with his parent visit, I loaded him in his car seat and went as fast as I could to the nearest Sonic. I ordered a cheeseburger, extra gluten, onion rings, a large drink, and an ice cream. And I gorged myself on these nasty items and cried. I worshipped at the feet of a supersized value meal. When I was finished, I had heartburn, guilt, self-disdain, and mustard on my shirt. The world was no better off from my behavior.

Idol worship.

I instantly wanted a do-over. I had missed an opportunity to be comforted by my heavenly Father. I lost a chance to sit at His feet and hear, directly from Him, how much He loved that baby girl and how He grieved for this misguided family. I missed the chance to cry out to Him to intervene on her behalf, although I know He didn't need me to ask. I was sadder now than when I was held captive in that waiting room. This much I know: Idol worship is an open, oozing wound, and the only remedy is Real Jesus.

As I studied this I came to the conclusion: God knew this when He forbade idol worship in the Ten Commandments. He was aware that it would bring us nothing but heartbreak. I used to believe that God created the Ten Commandments to keep us in line, and to an extent, this may be the case, but I propose He made them primarily to protect us from ourselves, and then He died to free us from the burden of the law. The condemnation and burden of idol worship is no more, but the *conviction* of the division of my heart lingers. I wish I would never forget this lesson, but I already have, and I've done it again, a couple of times.

The further I traveled into the depths of my misunderstandings of Jesus, the more evident it became: He didn't expect me to overcome my idols. Not in the way I believed. On this occasion with the baby girl, I asked Him to please not only forgive me, but show me where I went wrong, besides the obvious, and how to be better. That evening I came across this scripture:

> Count it all joy, my brothers, when you meet trials of various kinds, for you know that testing of your faith produces steadfastness. And let steadfastness have its full effect, that you may be perfect and complete, lacking in nothing (James 1:2-4 ESV).

Satan is well at work in every aspect of my journey. If the enemy is messing with me, he is entirely intent on helping me screw up. I am continually reminded that his primary goal is to separate me from Jesus, just like in the garden. What this scripture says to me is that I should rejoice in the test. Like lifting weights, the test will strengthen me and enable me to stand up against it the next time and the next. I grieve the failure of the trial, but I rejoice that Satan thinks me an issue. I lament that I made myself sick and missed out on communing with Jesus, but I rejoice that He is a God who forgives and forgave; it is done. Now I grow in strength, like a baby learning to walk, when I stumble. *And in this, the revelation of who Jesus really is continues to unfold.*

The work was done on Calvary. The Real Jesus is waiting for me to come to Him. But the counterfeits still busy me. I am still searching screens, poking fun at Timberlake groupies and doll collectors, and chowing down on greasy comforts to compensate for what I am missing in a freedom walk with the Real Christ.

He wants so much goodness for me. He created me to know Him with my whole heart. He created me because He wanted my company, and He is jealous when I choose another. I imagined Him sitting at the foot of my bed that night after the scene at CPS. He was filled with the purest compassion. There in the midst of indigestion, regret, and sadness for a little girl in a new foster home and a family in desperate need of Him, I felt a bittersweet understanding of what it meant to live with Jesus wandering my halls, waiting for me to look up from obsessions. I was sorry He had been cast from my heart's focus, unrecognized by the busyness of my idol worship.

But the grandest revelation? He wasn't mad.

Before all the bad Jesuses were evicted from my life, my entire focus would have been on what a loser I was. How I was fat and pathetic. Alas, I knew those voices were not coming from Him. I was starting to recognize His voice now as unequivocally different. I pray you can decipher it well. It is gentle. It is compassionate. It is the expression of complete love.

I prayed, "Heavenly Father, help me keep me eyes on the real You. Let me not be fooled.

"Only on You..."

Oh, friend, He was about to unearth something in me.

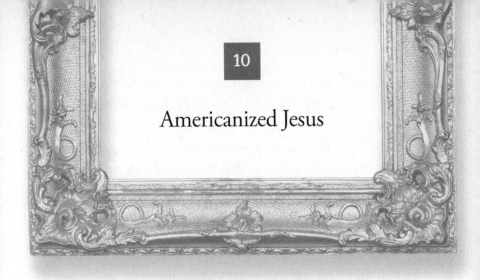

10

Americanized Jesus

*For the time is coming when people will not
endure sound teaching, but having itching
ears they will accumulate for themselves
teachers to suit their own passions.*

2 TIMOTHY 4:3 ESV

I have come to believe you cannot lose your salvation except in incidents involving FAFSA (Free Application for Federal Student Aid). If the fruit from the tree of good and evil thing hadn't worked on Eve, I feel confident Satan's plan B was to have her navigate government funding for Cain and Abel's university tuition.

On one particularly awful day, I had *three* applications in process. The Vandals, of course, were in rare form; all that really needs to be said here is they found the game cupboard. (If you ever want to play Monopoly at my house, be prepared to be able to spell your way out of jail, name the capital of Iowa to buy Park Place, and keep your right foot on red and your left hand on green if you want houses or hotels.) The scene also included a child playing the entire score from *Les Misérables* on the piano while singing at the top of her lungs, crying, and occasionally dipping Oreos in the peanut butter. Also, the foster child slumbering on my lap had rotavirus. Cue Cosette's "Castle on a Cloud" and please pass the Oreos.

And when the day was done, after I had finished digging the last of the Oreo crumbs out of the peanut butter jar, I climbed into bed hating everything about myself and believing the lies of the enemy. I'd screwed up. I'd botched everything important.

But I'd start over. *Next week.*

For the rest of *this* week, since I was already a failure, I would sleep past the alarm that was meant to wake me up for quiet time in my prayer chair. For the rest of this week I would eat Frosted Flakes, Oreos, and Pop Tarts for breakfast. This week I would skip Pilates and give up all hope of bodily perfection. This week I would eat Cheetos and watch reruns of *Friends*, and during the commercials I would write down my new goals in my brand-new *All Things Work Together for Good* journal with a purple pen. (Purple for royalty, because I would be a princess, daughter of the King, come Monday.)

Next week Jesus and I would be unstoppable.

But Monday came and things weren't better. And the next Monday, and the next.

Maybe you, too, have a Monday list? A list of all the ways you're going to be better next week. But you try and you try and still things aren't better.

You'll never be good enough for Americanized Jesus. There's too much to do. Too much to be. No one could serve a master who demanded so much.

"It's easy to break up with Americanized Jesus. It's impossible to break up with the Real Jesus."

That was the start of my journey, or at minimum when I became aware of the journey, all the way back at that writer's conference, and that Americanized Jesus was the last false savior to be slain. But the Real Jesus never gave up on me. The first time I heard His name, He joined me and showed me, most lovingly, *Nope, let's keep going.* Still, the loudest Jesus, the one furthest from the Real Christ, was the one who served me best yet always made me feel less.

Americanized Jesus is the one I call on when I need my cappuccino to have just the right amount of foam, when I think I can't face another day unless I get my Swedish massage. He's the one I beg to wipe away the carbs and fat grams from my extra-large plate of fettuccini Alfredo. (And I am mortified that I need to whine about this. The size of my bum is truly a first-world issue that should be easily resolved with some self-control, which is an attribute of the fruit of the Spirit, if only I would try harder. Americanized Jesus and I chatter about it often. I am readily ashamed.)

Americanized Jesus comes bearing Italian leather with seat warmers and leaves a giddy, fuzzy feeling after I sing loud praise-and-worship songs. And I propose that this is a key factor in missing out on the Real Jesus. From the self-inflicted guilty comfort of my elaborate home, Jesus had been harder to find. Further from my reach. I was distracted. I was spoiled. I had a Jesus Fish watermark on my checks, and I gave my exact ten percent. And in return, I expected Jesus to grant my wishes for ease and affluence.

I got so caught up in my comfort zone that my prayers were empty lists of wants and wishes. I had minimized Him, friends— turned Him into nothing more than a genie in a bottle. Where two or more are gathered, yes, He is there, but that doesn't translate to *where two or more are gathered He will give me a Lexus.* And where two or more are gathered doesn't mean life won't still hurt. It just means He will be there when it does.

Hardworking Holiness

Recently, a friend of a friend—a youth minister—was looking for summer mission work for his well-to-do tweens and teens. His e-mail request was forwarded to me:

> Families, we are looking for a way for our youth to serve this summer and increase in faith. We will be painting a Sunday school classroom at a church in a "less than" neighborhood. We will go out for dinner afterward. If you would like to sponsor one of our youth's dinners, we are going to a local restaurant for an all-you-can-eat Nacho Night.

It gets worse.

A close friend whose husband recently left the ministry implored me to share their last straw. After driving to a mountain church camp, this young youth pastor began to receive seething phone calls from two of the campers' families. The minister and his wife had been provided with a real bed and a private bath with a toilet, sink, and meager shower. The student campers were in bunks with a communal bathroom. The parents of these students demanded that their children be treated with the same "luxuries" afforded the youth minister. One of the mothers came and retrieved her child in the middle of the night when the minister didn't comply. Upon returning to the home church, the youth minister was forced by elders to apologize to the family for denying the child "common comforts."

Another friend shared that after an "intense and physically challenging" inner city mission, her four students climbed in the church van utterly exasperated. She overheard one of the sweaty girls say, "That was good for me. I needed the reality check."

To which her friend replied, "Yeah, and now I need a manicure and to never come back to this disgusting hole."

My friend lamented, "They aren't bad kids. They have heard and believed in the name of Jesus. Still, they think they're above any kind of work, any kind of service for the kingdom."

American Christians, we are ridiculous.

The starving, the broken, the dying, the orphaned, the refugee, the sick, the suffering—I am pretty sure Real Jesus is most concerned with the least of *these*. If I have to face my God today, let it be said of me that I gave the last ounce of myself to a child in need.

Jesus told us to love. But we make our love conditional on our convenience. We do the Lord's work as long as it doesn't hurt and we get some fun reward afterward. While a real-life girl carries her meager belongings from foster home to foster home in a trash bag, we plant some daisies at the church and then head to the all-you-can-eat buffet, patting ourselves on the back all the way through the line. We're impressed by our hardworking holiness.

Here is a confession: I got into foster care thinking I could trick God.

All I really had was a horrified spirit—horror at the mistreatment of children—but I wanted God to think I had a servant's heart. I wanted to serve the "least of these," but I gave myself an out clause: We became a "foster to adopt" family. That way we wouldn't get hurt.

When the caseworker called about our first placement, I listened intently as she described a wounded, abused baby boy lying in a hospital bed, needing someone to cuddle him. And the first words out of my mouth?

"Is he adoptable?"

The caseworker paused. "I don't know, Jami," she said. "But he's terribly hurt, and he's here all alone."

Me and my holiness. Worrying so much about myself and my own heart that I was tempted to ignore a child in need.

Missionary used to be a big word. It meant an undeniable calling on your life. The Kent Brantlys of the world, who laid down their lives for the gospel and held the hands and washed the bodies of the victims of Ebola, were the missionaries. Now the car wash by the youth group to raise funds for a trip to a splash park gets the same label.

Back at the church, the music keeps getting louder and louder, and the pastor is expected to provide our youth with an HD religious experience that can compete with their media-addicted brains every time they walk in the door. (As if pastors are responsible for entertaining our spirits.) Not to mention he needs to be politically correct if he wants the collection plates full. Speak out against the wrong thing or preach on those inconvenient truths found in Scripture, and there will be an exodus of epic proportions. And if I don't "feel it," Jesus must have turned from me, because I have let Him down.

Lies.

I had mistaken Real Jesus for a wealth of characters that I molded together to meet my specific needs. And those needs seemed unreachable from my wretchedness. So desperate to get back to the essence of the God I was created to worship, I had gone to great lengths to figure Him out, to solve the mysterious puzzle. I bought every single new book or study. I clawed my way to the front of the stadium to get the autograph from the great-teacher-du-jour. I trampled children to paw at the wise spiritual guru (whose bestselling book was on sale for just $29.99). And then I was utterly destroyed when they weren't Jesus.

I have heard it said and I've said, "I won't set foot back in a church." If I feel that way, well then, the people let me down...not Jesus. And how did they let me down? Did they lie? Cheat? Steal? Did they disagree with my stance on gay marriage? Or did they just forget to invite my kid to the back-to-school swim party? Guess what, Jami? They did that because they are human. And at this point in my journey, one thing was crystal clear: Humans can no longer be the deciding factor in the walk of relationship with Jesus. Okay, Jesus, but then how do I get it? How can I know Real Jesus?

I wanted specific directions on how to get this done. "Siri, how do I develop an intimate and deep-rooted relationship with the Jesus who died for me so that I might have eternal life?"

She didn't answer.

The Worst

I was up late one night, unable to sleep, scrolling through my news feed while Justin slept beside me. And a picture popped up—a little boy, about three years old, somewhere in the wild, in Africa. He'd been left there by his family, who believed him to be a witch. This is a common practice in the culture if a baby's top teeth come in before their bottom teeth. He was rescued by some local missionaries. The image of a young woman giving the rescued boy a drink of water left me reeling. The boy's image is burned in my heart; he was naked, nearly starved, and wounded.

You've seen pictures like this too.

I lay awake that night and wrestled with Americanized Jesus and Real Jesus. I thought about a little boy wandering in the wilderness with no mommy. I thought about my first-world struggles: I want a clean house and size-5 jeans, and I can't even go to the grocery store without losing my skirt or getting my hair tangled in a basket. I know—*poor Jami.* What is that in comparison to a little boy who is terrified and starved?

In my selfish prayers, in my self-important do-gooding, do I think Americanized Jesus cares more about me than that child? I sure act like I do sometimes. So in an effort to eradicate my guilt, I sign up to volunteer at comfy "missions" where nachos are the reward and I can count my deeds worthy.

I am the worst. I wish this were the Christian battle cry: "We are the worst!" The great, righteous apostle Paul said this himself: "Christ Jesus came into the world to save sinners—of whom I am the worst" (1 Timothy 1:15). The burdens, questions, and grief clawed at me as I watched the ceiling fan spin. I was out of tears and out of logic.

"It's easy to break up with Americanized Jesus. It's impossible to break up with the Real Jesus."

I got up and wandered once again to the prayer chair in front of Stolen Jesus. I sat grief-stricken and guilty. I prayed, "I will return and seek Your forgiveness. I will beg You to take me back...and we will continue the dance." I confessed, "I am so afraid of You." Tormented by a fire-and-brimstone Jesus that could not be placated, I cried out to Him and listed my fears. Fears I fully believed He would use to rein in my wayward, coffee-drinking, fat, wicked self for a more fruitful journey.

A new calm washed over me. *No, love.*

Chills erupted, and somehow, in that moment, I knew it would be different. I was on the verge of freedom. I heard it in my soul: He moves how He moves, He saves how He saves. I don't have to understand or explain Jesus. I just have to believe Him. That was the essence of the gospel of faith. Believing that what God said was true. I am righteous by the cross. The blood worked. Grace gave me eternity as the prize.

Oh, but we have Americanized Him—the Shepherd who appears to Muslims as they slumber, the Lion who speaks peace to the ages, and the Lamb who will go to slaughter for the herd.

The truth about Americanized Jesus was He was pompous. He was a *pay your dues, follow the rules, and I will bless you* Jesus. An if/then Jesus who turned toward me when I was good and turned away when I was bad. When I was good, I was puffed up with self-righteousness. And when I was bad, I was in danger of hell itself.

But I already had freedom. The work of the cross was complete. I just hadn't grasped the truth. Grace was banging on my door, but before I fully received it there was one thing left I felt I had to do: go head-to-head with the prince of lies.

11

Real Satan

Blessed are those whose transgressions
are forgiven, whose sins are covered.
Blessed is the one whose sin the Lord
will never count against them.

ROMANS 4:7-8

We live on a 640-acre ranch in West Texas. This has many blessings. Country living means the Vandals roam free and the stars at night are big and bright. However, it has its issues too. There are rattlesnakes, ground wasps, badgers, hogs, and packs of wild dogs.

People don't realize the gravity of the dogs. They are dangerous. Once on a walk with the kids, we had a close encounter with a pack of dogs. One of my dearest friends, Marcy, lived on land a mile from our ranch. A homeschool mom of four, Marcy and I would often get the kids together or create a "P.E. class" on the county road between our homes.

Everything about the horror of that day is burned into my mind. John and Luke were on their bikes ahead of me; my daughter

Maggie, Marcy, and her daughters were with me. The dogs came out of the brush, and John and Luke were face-to-face with them. I don't know what my friend and I thought we could do when we got there, but we ran toward them. One of the beasts latched on to John's leg. Our screams and the barking must have alerted a neighbor, who came running to our rescue and started shooting.

The dogs are dropped off by people who don't want them anymore. Oftentimes they are large-breed dogs. People think they are cute as puppies, and then they turn into massive brutes, so their owners dump them out here. Not only are they dangerous for the country-dwelling humans, but they have also been known to kill calves and chickens, run off deer, and eradicate the quail population. It is a shame, but there isn't really much to be done about it. Unfortunately, when necessary, we kill them and bury them in a pit where nature takes its course. (Please refrain from hostile e-mails; I am not the humane society. I know it is horrible.)

Recently, on a walk on the county road, my sister, who lives with her husband and children on our ranch, reported there was a terrible "death" smell by the bridge over the creek. The smell was so intense she was forced to cut her walk short and head in the other direction. A few days later my husband said he drove over the bridge. He was afraid it was a cow based on the magnitude of the smell. Still, none of us thought much about it. The next week my sister attempted to walk her regular route, and this time her dogs were tagging along for the jaunt. As she neared the bridge, she realized the smell was still very much an issue. Before she could turn around, her two dogs jumped the fence and headed to the creek. She covered her nose and began to holler for her dogs to come back, but they were on to the scent and couldn't be swayed to return.

The dogs found what they were looking for, and then the smell went from bad to worse. My sister's dogs had torn open a large black trash bag, which contained the remains of two dogs. The dogs had been killed, stuffed in a bag, and thrown off the bridge, which landed partially on the creek bank and partially in the creek. In the 104-degree June heat, the remains had turned into death soup.

All of us were terribly bothered by the scenario. It was just, well, despicable. And it occurred to me the dogs in the bag were an excellent picture of what the enemy has done to our relationship with the Real Jesus and sin.

Sin in its simplest form is that which separates us from God. The wages of sin is death (Romans 6:23). With death comes decay. And before we took on our new life in Jesus, our sin slowly ate away at us—just like the heat destroyed the bodies of those dogs we found in the bags. And sooner or later, the result of our sin would be our eternal death. But Christ's work on the cross purchased us eternal life.

And we think, *Surely we must earn this.* We must earn everything else in this society. Trophies (except outfielder trophies), grades, pay raises, promotions, and praise are accolades we must work to achieve. But we would be wrong, because all the Clorox in the world can't wash away the death soup of our sin.

Satan's Master Plan

My dearly departed mother-in-law gave Satan credit for everything. *Everything.* Like the day when, in the grand family tradition of Something Must Go Wrong, my son got his head stuck in a fence at the zoo. Twice. He stuck his head between the bars and couldn't get it back out. Zoo maintenance came and pried the bars open and pulled his head out. Two exhibits down, he did it again. I was half tempted to leave him, but the maintenance guy came again, and we went ahead and counted that as a full day at the zoo.

When we got home, our failed Houdini and his genius brother decided to build a "bike ramp." The disastrous duo dug a three foot by three foot *hole* in the ground, about two feet deep. They took their bikes up the hill and then raced down toward the hole in the hopes of getting some "air."

At the hospital, my mother-in-law showed up to pray for us. She also brought a little bag of snacks and some crossword puzzles as we would be there awhile for stitches, skin grafts, and casts. This was very sweet. In the course of our prayers and conversation, she said the usual: "God love you! The devil is really after you today!"

Actually, I propose I am just the mother of sons. Dashingly handsome, strong-willed, not-so-bright sons. Sons living in a fallen world. I am blessed by them. They make me laugh. They make me cry. They make me question whether they will ever be able to function in society. Justin and I are proud, most days, to call them our sons. We do our best to teach them right from wrong and instill in them a desire to seek Real Jesus on their own.

And that is where I believe the enemy is most interested in interfering. Not in failed attempts to get a better look at the monkey exhibit, poorly executed bike stunts, or botched trips to Target. I believe he is more interested in the eternal cessation of the Christian species and holding us hostage from our true inheritance. He wants to keep us in bondage—bondage to the old covenant—and prevent us from walking in the light of our salvation. He's a dangerous enemy, but his tactics are simple: use the everyday frustrations of life to make us bitter, twisting our attitudes about our Savior.

So I don't think Satan was goading my sons into their injuries. But the fight over the hospital bill that Justin and I had a month later—yep, Satan was there for that. We were nothing short of ugly and sinful toward each other. I believe the enemy provoked and encouraged this behavior. As beings with free will, Justin and I could have chosen a higher road. We just didn't.

I worry that if I am constantly muttering, "That was an attack from the devil," I picture him down in the bowels of hell with a creepy, arthritic claw scratching tally marks on a cave wall, his grainy smoker's voice muttering, "Got her again," then I am giving him far too much attention. And I don't want him to have the pleasure.

I am certain, especially here in the Bible Belt, that we have embraced this verbiage excessively. Maybe it's because we want someone or something to blame. When our kid's football team loses at State, we say, "Jimmy, the devil doesn't want you to get that scholarship, so he threw the game." Jimmy lost the game, and everyone on the team blames Beelzebub. And poor Jimmy thinks to himself, *But we prayed before the game. I begged Jesus to let me win. He must not have been there for me.* And guess who wins now? Satan. He didn't even have to lift a finger. He just inadvertently separated poor Jimmy from the belief that Jesus was for him.

The visiting team prayed too. What about them? Their prayers were answered, and they won. So obviously Jesus was a Panther fan and not a Bulldog fan. Right? Thinking through this scenario helped me unravel a paramount lie: the belief that when I don't get my way, Jesus has turned His back on me. And Jesus turning His back on me is the very definition of terror.

When we are so flippant concerning the dark one, we actually further his reach. Satan is real, and he wants to break you up with Real Jesus. He wants you to believe untruths, and he wants you to be discontent with your current walk. He accomplishes this by whispering bitter awfulness in your ear. He is a liar, and he lies to separate me and you from the truth.

It is very easy to listen to those lies and become paralyzed by them. But instead, I pray that my brothers and sisters in Christ and I will remember the truth that God says we are made in His image. We are complex, and what I know now is we are all His chosen; He chose us to be with Him. Chosen and created by a jealous God. A

God who loves us unto death on a cross! And the enemy does not want you to begin the process of embracing this, so he lies. I rebuke the lies of the enemy and listen only to the truth of Scripture. Some days I feel I battle the enemy like a four-year-old, sending him to time-out over, and over, and over, and over.

I believe the enemy uses the nonsense in my mind to play a world of tricks. But I also know I am a sinner and that I mess up fairly well on my own. And while a lack of patience that causes me to yell is not from Jesus, I feel owning those actions as my sin, rather than claiming an attack from the dark side, is the responsible thing to do. Pawning my ickiness off on the devil is a cop-out. "The devil made me do it" sure doesn't convey a spirit of true repentance.

I think Satan pushes my buttons and uses my shortcomings to encourage further sin. However, I am not convinced that he is the mastermind behind my forgetting my wallet and forcing Justin to stop his work to bail me and my three hundred dollars' worth of groceries out of Walmart jail. I do believe how Justin and I respond to that inconvenience can be used by the devil to perpetuate sin. But I don't think that part of Satan's master plan for casting me into a fiery eternity involves forgetting my wallet on the kitchen counter.

Furthermore, while I believe the devil is the playwright of cancer, stomach bugs, wasps, and wickedness, I don't want him to receive any exceptional kudos. I try to mention him only when I am casting him to the foot of the cross. After all, as Romans 8:31 puts it—if God is for me, who can be against me? I might not recognize the restoration as I am walking through the valley of the shadow of death, but my reality doesn't change: He is with me.

Jesus Plus Nothing

Satan doesn't want me to know Real Jesus. He'd be quite content for me to continue believing in Mormon Jesus, or Fifth-Grade

Jesus, or Americanized Jesus, or any other savior who doesn't really save. Yes, I believe the evilest and most dangerous thing the enemy aspires to do is to get me to believe that Jesus is something He is not. Satan wants me to believe every lie and every wicked thing about the Son of Man that he can come up with—to believe that He is out of my reach and out to get me. The enemy wants me to imagine Jesus as harsh and full of condescending judgment. The devil may not have my soul for eternity, but he will try to convince me that I must somehow earn the grace that was purchased for me on Calvary. He wants me to believe that I must perform a certain way to earn my Creator's love, thereby providing me with a lifetime of torment.

So I performed. I gave my ten percent. I knelt to pray. And the enemy mocked my skimpy efforts and tightened the noose around my neck.

We need Jesus plus nothing. Jesus plus blogs, Jesus plus Bible studies, Jesus plus books, Jesus plus podcasts, Jesus plus grown-up coloring books...all of that is just extra. Not bad, just extra. You can have every scripture memorized and know every hymn by heart, but that doesn't change the utter simplicity of the fact that Jesus did the work. He died for our sins that we might live with Him for eternity, and it's really as easy as that.

When I look back over my beliefs about Jesus, I am more than willing to give credit to the enemy for the mind games he played with me. The enemy did his part to help create the Jesuses I worshipped and feared. He twisted human manifestations to appear holy when, in fact, they were far from it.

While I believe the devil likes to mess with us, I think we also give him too much credit. There's spiritual warfare, and then there's just *stuff*. Ordinary, everyday, *I live in this world and sometimes I have a bad day* stuff. If I call every blister, every flat tire, every scheduling mishap an attack of the enemy, I'm afraid he will take even more liberties. And our tendency to attribute these things to Satan can do damage to our witness when we post these thoughts on social media.

Yes, I know you can ask God for anything, but remember when you post it on Facebook, everyone sees it. So your urgent prayer request for extra queso on your nachos could be in the newsfeed of a nonbeliever who just got home from burying her two-year-old daughter. Won't the enemy be successful in constructing walls between believers and nonbelievers if we expose our hearts as this...shallow?

Furthermore, we say things like, "I am terrified for the future of our country." And nonbelievers are left to wonder, *How can they be terrified for the future of their country if they believe God is in control?*

The devil loves to take advantage of our fears and even our inconveniences. If you're terrified for our country, by all means, pray without ceasing. Yes, do that. In private. If your cable is out, pray it comes back on, but don't take down Christendom with the notion that this need is urgent. Babies are starving to death. You can catch *The Bachelor* on Hulu or YouTube. Let's all get a grip.

And it's not just what we post on social media. It's what we do. It's how we behave when we bear the name *Christian.* We slap Jesus fish on our cars and run red lights. Or we smack a sticker on our bumper that says, "In the case of rapture this car will be empty," and then we back into a Volvo while texting. From the comfort of our La-Z-Boys, we sign petitions about the things that offend us. We rant about what we fear. And we shout out ridiculous prayers, blaming the devil for his semi-wickedness interfering with our first-world living. I recently opened Facebook and saw an "Urgent prayer request..." A woman's cable was out, and she wanted prayers she wouldn't miss her show.

Stop it.

These images of us make a mockery of the cross, and we

perpetuate this with mini-rants for all the world to see. And the enemy sits back and watches in delight as we do all the work for him.

We must stop stealing Real Jesus.

Yes, we as Christians are often the thieves, stealing Jesus from both believers and nonbelievers. Of all the Jesuses I created in my mind, how many were fashioned by believers? More to my horror, what have I done or failed to do that invoked an imaginary Jesus persona to an acquaintance or loved one?

Believers, when we fight among ourselves, Satan just loves that. A prime example in homeschool circles is the debate over the age of the earth. But the age of the earth doesn't have anything to do with the message of the cross. We can argue about radiometric dating until we're blue in the face. It doesn't change what Jesus did. The argument just further distracts us and others from the Good News.

If we are continually bickering, posting, and ranting about a million different religiosities, opinions, and the one hundred reasons we don't celebrate Halloween, we aren't rejoicing in the fact that Jesus has risen. Time and again our freedom in Christ is trampled by our egos. The only one applauding is Satan.

"Well done. Thanks for making things so easy for me."

We are doing it wrong.

We are missing out on Jesus.

I can't walk perfectly, but Jesus doesn't ask me to. He invites me to come and rest. Jesus died for you that you might know Him and that His name would be made known. Cast the enemy to the foot of the cross, and then sit alone and *rest*, asking Him to reveal His whole, real self to you. Exactly where you are, exactly in the midst of your beliefs, right or wrong. Ask Him to convict you and strengthen you so you might overcome every attack or lie that Satan throws your way.

Under the law we had the primary sins—no god or idols; no

taking the Lord's name in vain; no adultery, false testimony against a neighbor, lust, forgetting the Sabbath, and so on. And that's the law. And then Jesus suffered, died, and was buried, and then on the third day He rose again. The new covenant set us free from the law. To hear us tell it, we need only believe, and we are saved. We get baptized, and we are washed in the water, and we are a new creation. Before when we messed up, did something that made us feel bad, something we knew in our core was bad for us, whether body, soul, or both, we had no hope. Under the new covenant, there is no condemnation, yet we have utterly distorted the message.

Yes, we were awful. We *needed* a Savior.

Jesus came and conquered.

The moment I realized Jesus's voice wasn't one of chastisement, I was undone. I can't tell you how elated and heartbroken I was at the same time. I hadn't been able to hear Him over the clever lies of High School Jesus, Scare-Me-Up Jesus, and all the rest. The reason I kept seeking baptism and forgiveness was that I hadn't actually embraced the entirety of the crucifixion. I was chained to the old covenant, believing the Holy Spirit was only there to help me conquer the law time after time.

In doing so, I had created an idol out of my own sin. I talked about it and read about it. I begged God to set me free from it. And then every day I took it back and wallowed in it. I obsessed over it and bought study after study to overcome it. I carried the death soup around in a black bag with a cross embroidered on the front. But as a dear friend told me, sin "doesn't need more prayer and more healing. You need only accept that which was already done on Calvary." The decay followed me because I didn't believe in the power of the cross. My focus was on the sin and how to manage it. This method of covering up and trying to contain it put the focus on that which I wished to escape!

In the simplest form, in toddlerish baby talk, I needed to relearn the Good News.

> Jesus loves me—He who died
> Heaven's gate to open wide;
> He will wash away my sin,
> Let His little child come in.

Real Jesus was here.

It was done.

And I was so relieved, so overcome with joy. The prodigal son wasn't the issue—the other son was. I rushed again to my prayer chair and flipped to the familiar tale in my Bible. And I fell to my knees, utterly undone by the revelation.

Perhaps the paramount work of the evil one lies in his ability to not only make us believe we must be "more" so as to earn the work accomplished on the cross but also to make us feel grand...as if we truly contributed. Oh, but he is maniacal. We can get sucked in to his darkest work—the demolition of the greatest story ever told—by making it about us rather than Jesus.

12

Just Jesus

*Having the eyes of your hearts enlightened,
that you may know what is the hope to
which he has called you, what are the riches
of his glorious inheritance in the saints.*

EPHESIANS 1:18 ESV

Our oldest Vandal, Sam, is an utter delight. We met him for the first time when he was just ten days old. He had no name, but the translator, a young woman from Canada who ran the nonprofit organization where Sam's birth mother sought help, coined the nickname "little man." Indeed, he had an aura about him that was indicative of an old soul.

In the days before we could get to him, the translator—who went well beyond her calling—and a foster family loved "little man" perfectly. Still, I cannot stand that I didn't know him sooner. And when I held him for the first time and stroked his silky, jet-black hair, kissed his caramel skin, and gazed into the blackest eyes I'd ever seen, I whispered a promise in his ear:

"Samuel Michael, I promise to take very good care of you. I will be the very best mommy your birth mother prayed for."

And I meant it. As happy as I was about this tender new life, I grieved for a scared woman who spoke no English and had no means to care for the angel now in my arms. When Sam cried in the night and I rushed to him, it was as much for her as it was for him. As he grew and it was time for him to sleep through the night, try as I could to let him find some comfort on his own, I could hear her imaginary voice, thick with a Spanish accent, reminding me, *Pero me lo prometiste...*

"But you promised me."

To date, Sam still gets up several times a night. I know, I am the worst. The funny part (well, not funny at 3:00 a.m.) is his attitude about his nighttime wanderings. As if he somehow remembers the promise, he comes to our room with righteous indignation. "Mommy! I am out of water 'cause you didn't get me more." Or "Mommy, I had a badder dream than ever 'cause you weren't wif me!"

The accusatory tone is wasted on my husband, who thinks he is just being rude and needs a bustin'. And it has expanded to other aspects of Sam's daily life. A couple weeks ago Sam and his partner in crime, Charlie, dumped a two-pound bag of sugar in the toilet. As I reprimanded them, Sam spouted off, "We gots in trouble 'cause you wouldn't let us play on the iPad." Granted, this is much different from the middle-of-the-night need of comfort. But I think he remembers—I promised him something. A verbal covenant between me and little man.

A Beautiful Shadow

My friend Tracy Levinson defines *covenant* as "a binding agreement or promise between two or more parties." And she goes on to explain that we aren't "throwing out the Old Testament or the law. The Mosaic Covenant is a beautiful shadow intended to direct us into the arms of our Savior. Although I respect Jewish law, it does not apply to me as a Christian. Jesus fulfilled it."[1]

Romans 7:6 states, "Now that we're no longer shackled to that domineering mate of sin, and out from under all those oppressive regulations and fine print, we're free to live a new life in the freedom of God" (MSG).

But the next Scripture reference is the one that pushed me out of the prayer chair and onto my knees. Hebrews 8:13 says, "When God speaks of a 'new' covenant, it means he has made the first one [Mosaic law] obsolete. It is now out of date and will soon disappear" (NLT).

Before we kick Mosaic law to the curb, it is imperative we understand what covenant is. And covenant is a much bigger deal than I have ever given it credit for. God dealt in blood covenants, which is an even bigger deal. A verbal covenant is just a word; a blood covenant requires a life.

Stop for a moment and ponder the weight of a life...the first time you held your child or the hand of a loved one as they passed on. Life is weighted.

I once accidentally killed our son Luke's guinea pig. In classic Jami fashion, I somehow convinced myself that Murphy the guinea pig needed fresh air. I still defend this decision. What on earth is a guinea pig, anyway? Do they travel in herds? Graze? Migrate? Hibernate? Granted, I have never seen or heard of a guinea pig being caught in the wild, but I felt it cruel for Murphy to spend his days in a cage next to Luke's smelly laundry basket, math homework, and Lego Pirate Cove. So a few times a week I would take him outside and put him under a wire mesh cage designed for baby chicks that I bought at the feed store.

Murphy seemed to enjoy his time outside. I would move him to different sections of the grass, and if it was too sunny I would move his entrapment under a cedar tree. By my own labeling, I believed myself to be the most considerate and wise guinea pig owner in the county. Well, until one Tuesday when he made his most daring escape. I will interject that I found it irritating that he was attempting to get out of his little cage. How many other guinea pigs get to even go outside? And the bottomless enclosure afforded him "mother earth" contact with grass and dirt. But the ungrateful beast figured out he could slip under the edge and roam the yard.

As if Murphy didn't already owe me a nod of worship for my generous efforts to bless him with "yard time," I saved him from a brutal death by barn cats. I had snatched Murphy up just in the nick of time and reprimanded the tailless rodent, "MURPHY D'WAYNE AMERINE!" (He was named after my husband's cousin.) "You cannot get out of your cage, mister! I don't have time for these shenanigans! I have to teach Latin to the kids, but when I come back you had best be in this cage!" I decided to put something heavy on top of the mesh enclosure, hoping it would keep him in the safe grass away from the feral felines now lurking in the cedar tree, staring down on the juicy guinea pig, licking their lips.

I spied a case of shotgun shells on the back porch. (What? We live on a ranch. Where do you keep your shotgun shells?) The box was wrapped in red plastic, but the plastic was torn, as Justin had opened the case and removed one box of shells. I set the box on top of Murphy's outdoor wonderland and went into the house to finish school with the children.

An hour later we came out to eat lunch on the picnic table. Murphy was on his back, legs up, roadkill position. I tried to revive him. A large portion of the red plastic from the shotgun shell case was gone. In his mouth was a tiny piece of the red wrapping. The plastic had either poisoned him or he had choked to death. Justin refused to pay for an autopsy.

As I wrapped his little body in a purple bandanna for burial, the weight of his lifeless carcass and my folly broke my heart—and that was an accident, just a rodent. For decades God's covenant with His people was based on the bloody sacrifice of animals. The very best animals. And when that proved fruitless, He made the ultimate covenant, one that couldn't be broken, with the purest sacrifice—Himself.

Ponder the weight of this.

In the old covenant or Mosaic law, the Word, which is holy, was a *written list* of what to do and what not to do. So this covenant between God and His people was a good method for the Jews to stay in line with God's heart, knowing what was good and what was bad. Just before Moses went to receive the commandments, the people promised to obey *all* the Lord said (Exodus 19:8). And then, immediately after Moses left, they crafted a lovely golden calf to keep them company.

The problem with the written law wasn't God—it was the people. That first bite of forbidden fruit continues to be the hill we die on. Over and over, we do the things we are told not to do. With the consistency of a three-year-old, I am told to stay out of the cookie jar, and yet I can't keep my hands out. So I experience the natural consequences of my actions, I repent, and I promise never to do it again.

Until I smell the cookies.

And round and round I go. The prophet Jeremiah predicted that there would be a time when God would make a new covenant (Jeremiah 31:31-33). This new covenant would someday be written on believers' hearts. When something is written on your heart versus written in stone, the Spirit is the guiding factor, and if you accept Jesus Christ into your heart, whose Spirit will guide you?

Right, *His.*

Guided by Spirit

I love donuts. In the tiny town about five miles from our ranch, there is a precious donut shop where the owner makes incredible hot and gooey yeast donuts. I could eat two dozen of them. You can smell them from the post office a mile away, and people come in droves for these tasty wonders. My husband drives into town every Monday through Friday to check the mail and then stops in the donut shop and gets (hopefully you are sitting down) ONE PLAIN CAKE DONUT. Justin is naturally thin. He could eat as many of the piping hot treats as he wants. Still, he gets one plain cake donut. This is foreign to me, so I finally asked him about it. And he said, "The other ones make me feel bad. I get heartburn, and they don't hold me over until lunch. Besides, *it's just breakfast.*" Aside from the fact I think he needs counseling, I recognize what is going on here: He is free from the law of *do not taste.*

So I decided to try this approach: I told myself that I can have as many of those donuts as I want. There is no condemnation in Jesus. If I want two dozen, I can have two dozen. I am free. One Saturday morning I drove to town for donuts for my family. On the way I contemplated how many I would eat and how many miles I would need to walk to burn them off my thighs. All of a sudden it wasn't just my thighs. Thoughts of indigestion, lethargy, joint pain from the gluten, and intestinal distress came into focus. Everything is permissible; not everything is beneficial (1 Corinthians 6:12). Rebellion against the law morphed into a heart change—*I don't want.*

Guess what else I don't want?

A plain cake donut. Because I am not a lunatic.

At my core I am still a normal human that doesn't understand plain cake donuts. But I opted for two eggs over medium and sprouted grain toast. I had a quarter of a donut for "dessert," but oddly enough, I decided it wasn't worth it and tossed it.

This is the transformation of the new covenant. Apart from the law, sin is dead (Romans 7:8). Paul asked, "Since you died with Christ to the elemental spiritual forces of this world, why, as though you still belonged to the world, do you submit to its rules: 'Do not handle! Do not taste! Do not touch!'?" (Colossians 2:20-21).

Now wanting what He wants isn't dreary. I still may want to eat a bag of Cheetos, but He who dwells in me guides me gently. I might have a handful, but I do so without condemnation or piety. I can have some. But I don't want to be a glutton because He is not a glutton. This is not an accomplishment on my part. I still have things I want, but conviction and freedom in knowing He did the work on Calvary changes the lingo. Now that I am in the captured love of God and a slave to righteousness, I want to walk in the freedom of a new mind. The new mind isn't obsessed with what is wrong with us; it is obsessed with what He has completed on Calvary.

I don't have to beg Him to set me free.

Because He already did.

Hebrews 8:10-12 (ESV) says:

> This is the covenant that I will make with the house of
> Israel
>   after those days, declares the Lord:
> I will put my laws into their minds,
>   and write them on their hearts,
> and I will be their God,
>   and they shall be my people.
> And they shall not teach, each one his neighbor
>   and each one his brother, saying, "Know the Lord,"
> for they shall all know me,
>   from the least of them to the greatest.

For I will be merciful toward their iniquities,
    and I will remember their sins no more.

But still, even under the new covenant, the battle unfolds.

The Brokenness

Recently a friend learned her husband had been cheating for eleven years. He was a church elder; his paramour was the church secretary. Their coconspirator and cover man: the music minister.

Brokenness.

Sex slavery, political corruption, child abuse, drug addiction, pornography, and all the other ills of the world God so loved...

And before I found Real Jesus, I attended to the tragedies. I sniveled at the brokenness. I beseeched God to illustrate His wrath. "How does this not incite Your mighty fury?" In my prayer chair in the black, I gave up. There was too much hurt. I waited for the truth, and one night it came like flashes of light and the cage-rattling eruptions of a Texas-sized tempest.

The room exploded with light as a rainstorm from the west crept over our ranch home. Blazes of light, and then incredible crashes of thunder, and still I waited. With each passing detonation of electricity and boom of unsearchable sound, I watched the face of Stolen Jesus appear and fade away. Friend, the outside forces, the power of darkness, could not change the absolute truth that Real Jesus was in the room. Even when the light is gone, He persists.

We are not toddlers. You can hide your head beneath a blanket, but I can still see the rest of you; I know you are still in the room. He does not change because of who we are in our brokenness, and He is the Great I Am no matter if we are sinning or doing good. Hating my neighbor, binging on yeast donuts, or lying to my kids about their participation in team sports...*He remains.* Adopt babies, move to a tent in Africa, sell everything you have, yell at your kids...*He remains*. Life is still life, cuts still bleed...*He remains*.

We can continue to walk in the shadow of the law. But what was purchased on the cross cannot be undone. And because of that purchase, I want what He wants.

Remember what Jesus said to the woman caught in adultery in John 8? "Go and sin no more" (verse 11 NLT). Why did He ask her to do the impossible? Because Jesus knew He would withstand the cross. It wouldn't be much longer. Love extended beyond the law of the Jews and the woman's ability to change her heart. Jesus didn't come to abolish the law. He came to fulfill it. He was aware that the adulterous woman would no longer be shackled to her past sins and failures. Her story would be made known when Jesus exalted her, a *daughter*.

She was made new. She would no longer hunger in the flesh. She would no longer crave filling up the hollow spaces with the adoration of men. Her heart was changed. And the church cries, "*Hallelujah!*"

Still, you ask, what now? What happens to the adulterer, the drug addicted, the child abuser, the home wrecker, and the glutton? Who is this God of the new covenant? His name is Jesus. He came to heal the sick and the suffering—we need only to believe.

As the storm rages, I storm heaven with the reality that Jesus is on the throne.

My prayers are new.

Bad things happen, good things happen. Still He remains.

I believe He will bind up the brokenhearted.

I believe He will make all things new.

Eve was given one rule. Just one. Still, she disobeyed. We've were given the whole law, and there's no way we could keep it. God knew that. He knew, and He knows our only hope would be for Him to lay down His life for us so that we could be free—free from the law and condemnation.

He came to fulfill the law. Under it, I may be convicted of my sin, but I will never again be condemned. Ask Him to remove the scales from your eyes. You needn't rush ahead: Jesus will meet you in the vestibule, and you will fully recognize His smile. He will hear your pleas from the barren floor of the Ebola ward in a makeshift hospital in Africa, and He will hear your pleas to move the line at Starbucks just the same. Not because of who we are, but because of how He loves.

Believing in the unseen restoration is so freeing. I was upset over a financial struggle recently. I started down the old road, picturing Jesus judging my poor management of funds and mocking me as I suffered. No, no, no. He is with me. He guides me peaceably. He is a gentle teacher, and He brings a refreshed mind, plans, and opportunities to right the wrongs.

Jesus doesn't give you a cloak that's been mended and given some stain treatments. No, He gives you a brand-new garment. He made it for you. It is gleaming white and sparkling clean. The Father sees us through the Son's eyes. Blameless.

You needn't fret over the future: It is done. Yes, imperfect people will challenge you, and they may succeed in hurting you, but you will not hurt alone. You don't have to have all the answers right now. Let Him reign. Leave Him on the throne. It is just fine to sit at His feet and merely whimper, "Be Jesus."

At the height of my struggle with my weight, I was beating my body into submission with as many as five hours of high-impact aerobics a day. Mass in the morning, insane workouts throughout the day, and observance of every single rule. In such bondage to my works, I had a laminated checklist and various colors of dry-erase markers by which I recorded and gauged my performance.

When my body could no longer withstand the pressure, I was terribly injured and forced to come face-to-face with the reality that nothing else could be done.

Hallelujah.

I can't do it. You can't do it. We are no longer responsible for fixing ourselves. The law no longer stings. And while you are coming to fully understand and embrace the new covenant and grace-filled living, naysayers and those in bondage to the law might ask you by what authority you believe you are free from the law. You need only answer, "Just Jesus."

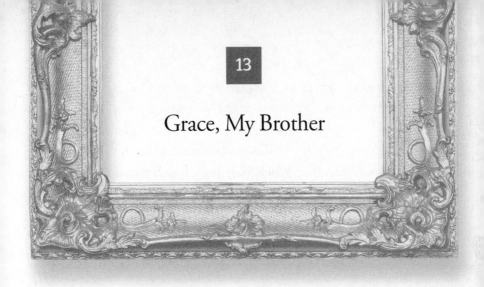

13

Grace, My Brother

*We are more than conquerors through
him who loved us. For I am convinced
that neither death nor life, neither angels
nor demons, neither the present nor the
future, nor any powers, neither height nor
depth, nor anything else in all creation,
will be able to separate us from the love
of God that is in Christ Jesus our Lord.*

ROMANS 8:37-39

Our two oldest biological sons, John and Luke, are eighteen
months apart in age. John, the elder of the two, failed his
hearing test at birth, so for a good portion of his infancy, we believed
he was deaf. Later we discovered he had an auditory processing
disorder—an umbrella diagnosis of dyslexia and other learning
disabilities.

Neither John nor Luke spoke. They had an odd little language
they used with each other, but no one else could understand it.

We understood that "Ya-Ya" meant Maggie and "nacky" meant gross, but otherwise it was like they were in their own little world.

When John was four and Luke was three, I took them for some testing at a nearby school. The boys were tested separately, apart from me and each other. When I sat down to hear the results, I was more confused by the outcomes than I was by their brother-speak. John had the vocabulary of a toddler. Luke had the vocabulary of a sixth grader.

Wait.

What?

"John doesn't talk," I agreed. "But Luke? He's never spoken."

"Yes, he *does* speak," the examiner insisted. I learned that Luke was, in fact, able to talk in complete sentences, and he knew the alphabet, numbers, colors, and shapes. But he had stayed under the cloak of his older brother's disabilities to remain in an unspoken bond.

Alone with Luke that night, lying beside him on the bottom bunk, I said, "You can talk to me." He looked at me, and a smile spread across his cherub face, dimples flashing. No words. And I said, "John will talk more if you talk to him." Luke's green eyes swelled. His lip quivered. And we both cried.

He didn't say anything.

Slowly, over the next few weeks, Luke started speaking more and more, and John followed quickly behind.

And now? They rarely shut up. But for so long, Luke lived in bondage to silence that was not his birthright, not his cross to bear.

Years ago a woman in our lives was having multiple affairs. The ongoing drama was mind blowing. At one point she had no less than three extramarital relationships going at once. She had five children under the age of seven. I was baffled by her endurance and her interest in recreational sex with strangers. Every Wednesday she came to Bible study, determined to overcome her sin. Sin that the rest of us didn't believe she had any interest in defeating.

One day I was dropping some out-of-town guests off at a hotel near our home. I saw this woman exit the hotel with an apparent lover on her arm. From my car I watched as she kissed him passionately, then she got in her car and made a phone call. After she hung up, she put her face in her hands and heaved heartbroken sobs.

Unable to break free from the bondage of the law.

Living out a life of lies.

Desperate and destroyed.

If I'd known then what I know now, I would have climbed out from the hiding place of my car and gone to her. I would have told her, "He died so you would no longer have to live like this. Not to work to overcome your sin, but to just believe that it is overcome. You drank from the water; you never have to thirst again. You are believing the lie that you are unforgiven and dirty. But you are forgiven and clean. When you realize that there is no law, that you are free to live like this and still He loves you—the bondage of sin shifts. You were made for more than this struggle. You are righteous." And today I tell you the same thing I should have told her:

You are not condemned.

You are not unsalvageable.

You are restored.

You are free.

What Happened in Sychar

The book of John, chapter 4, tells a story a lot like the one above—a story about bondage to the law. Jesus has just arrived in a town called Sychar, in Samaria. The town was near the land that Jacob gave his son Joseph, so Jacob's well was there. (I'm just imagining Jesus leaning over to read the historical marker beside the well—sort of like the ones my dad used to stop to see on long road trips.)

Jesus has been traveling around and teaching, but now He and His disciples are on the lam from persecutors. Jesus sits at the well, probably hot and tired, while His disciples go into town to buy food.

While He is resting on the edge of the well, a Samaritan woman comes along to draw water. Jesus asks her for something to drink, and she says, "You are a Jew and I am a Samaritan woman. How can you ask me for a drink?" Jews and Samaritans didn't speak because they believed in different religious laws. Samaritans worshipped the God of the Jews, but they didn't worship in the Jewish temple. Furthermore, they believed in only the first five books of Moses.

Jesus says to the woman, "If you knew the gift of God and who it is that asks you for a drink, you would have asked him and he would have given you living water."

And she says, "Sir, you have nothing to draw with and the well is deep. Where can you get this living water?"

Jesus says, "Everyone who drinks this water will be thirsty again, but whoever drinks the water I give them will never thirst. Indeed, the water I give them will become in them a spring of water welling up to eternal life."

She wants this water. She is dying of thirst—parched by the law of her forefathers and by the burden of her sin. Jesus goes on to reveal His knowledge of her sin—how she's lived with many men.

And then He declares Himself to be the long-awaited Messiah. He says, "I, the one speaking to you—I am he."

And this woman believes because she has met Jesus. She is different because she interacts with Him. He knows her, and in that encounter, she now has a Savior. When He leaves, He doesn't leave her a Bible, Scripture memory cards, highlighters, colored pens, crayons, a concordance, a tablet, or study lessons. He just leaves the knowledge of Himself.

She is left to ponder Jesus and how He knew her. It wasn't about her nationality or skin color. He didn't acknowledge her good deeds. He only forgave her the old sins.

This is grace. We sin. Jesus came for us, the sinners. He was a friend of the sinner and the Samaritan and the tax collector. And He had what they and we need.

Grace.

Lloyd and Larry

Still not convinced? Another story about bondage to the law. You can find this one in Luke 15:11-32. A very wealthy man has two sons—let's call them Lloyd and Larry. Larry asks for his inheritance now instead of later (rather than waiting until his father's passing), and his father gives it to him. Larry then leaves his father's house.

Lloyd stays home and continues to run his dad's business. The father grieves for Larry; he worries about his wellness, body and soul. Meanwhile, Larry eats, drinks, and parties with loose women. He blows through his inheritance and is soon homeless and unhappy, chowing down on pig slop to survive. Finally, contrite and fed up with the pauper's life, Larry decides to go home and see if his father will at least give him a job.

When the father sees Larry coming, he goes nuts. With no cell phones or Facebook updates, Larry's father is relieved to see his boy is alive and headed toward the house. He orders a feast to celebrate Larry's return and welcomes him home with nothing but love.

But Lloyd, the loyal brother, balks: "I am a pretty good kid. Still, you never slaughtered a fattened calf for me. You never threw my friends and me a banquet. I kill myself for you, and I get nothing!" He brags of his obedience and laments his lack of pay.

One brother ran free from law and rule and then begged to come home to the safety of that which was beneficial. The other brother was enslaved to that which was not required. And when older son voiced his complaint, his father said, "All I have is yours. Nothing was required of you. I just love you."

In my life, I have played the part of both brothers.

I never actually left my inheritance to squander it. I struggled, and will continue to struggle, with sin, like every human on the planet, but minus the short breakup, a large portion my life has been centered on the Father. Yet I threw the same tantrum: "I have done all the things I'm supposed to do. Still, the ends don't meet, the scale won't budge, and I can't get a moment of silence! What have You done for me?"

The Father replied, *All that I have is yours. You are always with Me.*

Instead of embracing the abundance He offered me, I chose to be worried and fitful. I lived as though among the pig's slop, with no hope of the freedom bought for me by the cross. I wandered the halls of my Father's house and stood outside the banquet hall but didn't go inside. I griped and complained outside the door of the feast (and listed my good deeds) and refused to accept the gift of my inheritance. *All He has is mine*, but I ignored my birthright.

Friends, I wholly believe that too many Christians are living out the old covenant. Here's how that old covenant life looks:

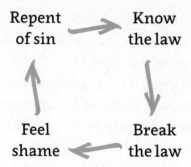

Know the law, break the law. That pattern started all the way back in the garden of Eden. Just one command—that was all Adam and Eve had to obey. But the flesh rebels against the law, and so sin entered the world.

God gave His people more rules, more laws to obey. You can read them for yourself in Scripture. There are hundreds of commands, which Jesus neatly summarized: "Love the Lord your God with all your heart and with all your soul and with all your mind...[and] love your neighbor as yourself" (Matthew 22:37,39).

We couldn't even do that.

Know the law, break the law. As Romans 3:23 puts it, "Everyone has sinned; we all fall short of God's glorious standard" (NLT).

A few months back I ran into Starbucks dragging my toddler sons—my dark-skinned Sam and my towheaded Charlie—and lugging a bulky car seat with a blue-eyed baby girl inside.

An older man made eye contact with me. I smiled. He rolled his eyes.

I heard his wife say, "My, she has her hands full."

And he scoffed and said, "Yeah, and looks like she's popular with a few fellas." And they laughed. He continued, "Glad our tax dollars can buy her a six-dollar cup of coffee."

Again they laughed.

By all appearances, it is safe to assume my children have different dads. But what made him think he was buying my coffee? I was slightly disheveled, but I hardly looked homeless.

I brushed it off. I moved on.

Diaper changes, hand washings, and a head injury later, Charlie was bandaged up and I had apologized profusely for the damage to the Caramel Macchiato display. We headed back to the car. As luck would have it, the older folks who had decided I was the welfare whore of Babylon were on our heels.

I pleaded with my sons to stay close. I awkwardly balanced my coffee while I hauled the bulky car seat to my car. I could feel their eyes on me. And I heard him say, "She hardly needs to be eating scones."

I disliked this guy.

(Also—this just needs to be said—I was not eating a scone.)

As I herded the kids into the car, Sam proceeded to karate chop and kick the blue Honda parked next to us with his tiny fists and feet. I barked, "Samuel Michael! No, sir!"

Yeah, it was their car.

I made my apologies, and they just stared. As I turned to my car, I heard the man say, "Well, that's our society for ya!"

And he would be correct. Our society judges by what we *think* we see and what we hold as truth when we have no idea what we're talking about.

The Vandals and the baby finally fell asleep as I drove, and I was left to ponder.

I am guilty of the same behaviors. No matter what he said about me, no matter what he believed, that man was my neighbor. Did I love him as I love myself? Did I give him the benefit of the doubt or know anything about his history and circumstances before I declared him a judgmental grump?

I was not only the recipient of the offense; I was the offender.

Later that night, as I tried to sleep, I couldn't shake the image of the man. He showed such disgust for what he believed my situation to be...and I was most horrified by the knowledge that *I have looked the same way.* I have judged harshly. I have been unwilling to listen to the intensity of a struggle. I have been so steeped in self-righteousness that I was incapable of seeing Christ in the least of these.

All have sinned.

Especially me.

As the apostle Paul put it in Romans 7:15, "I do not understand my own actions. For I do not do what I want, but I do the very thing I hate" (ESV). Jesus knew we couldn't keep the covenant.

The old covenant required payment for the forgiveness of sins: a blood sacrifice. The law was impossible to keep, so God's people had to make sacrifices in order to be cleansed of their unrighteousness and avoid His wrath. Jesus was the ultimate, final sacrifice. He was a sinless offering—fully man, but also fully God. This is the perfect romance—the perfect, selfless sacrifice that tore the veil between me and God.

> Greater love has no one than this: to lay down one's life for one's friends (John 15:13).

In sacrificing Himself, Jesus took the judgment for all people. Now our sins are forgiven. We no longer live as slaves to the law. Romans 8:1 declares, "There is now no condemnation for those who are in Christ Jesus."

There is only grace.

Grace.

Grace.

Grace.

Oh, friend, this is the grace.

Grace is the gift of the new covenant! The father of Lloyd and Larry wasn't stewing and plotting the destruction of Larry. He couldn't wait to lavish his love on his boy. When he saw him from afar, he ordered a feast, new clothes, and a grand welcome! Grace. "Come, feast, join in the abundance! What is mine is yours, my child."

I don't have to sleep with pigs when He has invited me inside.

Our Father has declared the struggle accomplished. This is the new covenant, that while we were still sinners, God sacrificed His only Son so that we could be made clean. Now, when you are in the throes of what you know isn't part of God's goodness, you are *convicted,* but not condemned. Moreover, when you are resting in the finished work of the cross, you want what He wants—you will desire what He desires.

I don't want to have torrid affairs with strange men at random hotels. I don't want to lust after the star of the latest Netflix drama. I don't want to yell at my kids after a small infraction. I don't want to snap at the cashier in the grocery store just because I'm having a rotten day. But do I do those things? Yes. (Not the torrid affair thing, just for the record.) As Paul wrote in Romans 7:18, "I have the desire to do what is good, but I cannot carry it out." I'm still playing Larry, running away from the Father as fast as I can. But with God's Spirit in me, my inner desire is for Him. I want what He wants.

Out from Underneath

I have struggled with my weight and a slew of eating disorders since I was twelve. With polished nails, whitened teeth, and Spanx upon Spanx holding this and that in unnatural configurations, I have obsessed over my outward appearance and begged God to make me different. The fruit of this was a stressed, unhappy, and enslaved woman, confined to the idea that I could never please God. (Also, I can remove Spanx in the most creative of fashions. I am notorious for taking them off and leaving them in random environments.)

But He was already pleased.

After He unearthed the roles I have played as both Lloyd and Larry, I was paralyzed with the fear, "What now?" What plan? What pill? What fat content? Carbs? Sugars? What rules do I follow?

So I waited for Him to tell me.

My stomach growled. I was hungry, but I stood at the fridge and didn't know what to eat. Giving up on the rules left me confused. Now what? What will I do with all my time if I am out from underneath the law?

Toast with butter and jam. Orange juice. And coffee with cream and real sugar.

For lunch I had a salad...with real Ranch and bacon bits.

Why did I ever believe full-fat Ranch was a sin? It is from Jesus! Again, the enemy muddies the waters and adds weight to the load. God's laws are holy and good. Just like my son Luke, just like my adulterous friend, just like the woman at the well, I had been living under a burden that was never mine to bear. No, I could never be perfect the way God commands. I keep on sinning; I keep messing up. But Jesus was perfect on my behalf. Jesus was perfectly obedient to God the Father's commands. And because of His obedience and sacrifice, I have been washed clean. His grace has changed everything.

Here's how the apostle Paul put it in his letter to the Romans:

> By entering through faith into what God has always wanted to do for us—set us right with him, make us fit

for him—we have it all together with God because of
our Master Jesus. And that's not all: We throw open our
doors to God and discover at the same moment that he
has already thrown open his door to us. We find ourselves standing where we always hoped we might stand—
out in the wide open spaces of God's grace and glory,
standing tall and shouting our praise...

Christ arrives right on time to make this happen. He
didn't, and doesn't, wait for us to get ready. He presented
himself for this sacrificial death when we were far too
weak and rebellious to do anything to get ourselves ready.
And even if we hadn't been so weak, we wouldn't have
known what to do anyway. We can understand someone
dying for a person worth dying for, and we can understand how someone good and noble could inspire us to
selfless sacrifice. But God put his love on the line for us
by offering his Son in sacrificial death while we were of
no use whatever to him.

Now that we are set right with God by means of this
sacrificial death, the consummate blood sacrifice, there
is no longer a question of being at odds with God in
any way. If, when we were at our worst, we were put on
friendly terms with God by the sacrificial death of his
Son, now that we're at our best, just think of how our
lives will expand and deepen by means of his resurrection life! Now that we have actually received this amazing friendship with God, we are no longer content to
simply say it in plodding prose. We sing and shout our
praises to God through Jesus, the Messiah! (Romans 5:1-
2,6-11 MSG).

It is too good to be true—no, it is so good it *must* be true.
And now Real Jesus is coming into focus.

I imagine myself sitting at a desk. The paper in front of me is just a cartoon of Jesus, and the teacher walks in and hands me a brand-new box of crayons. I smell them—there's nothing like the smell of new crayons.

I look up at Stolen Jesus. "What color are You?" I ask.

Red for the blood.

White for the redemption.

Green because I am jealous of the time you spent worshipping someone or something else.

Hot pink for the celebratory dance as you opened the door to the banquet hall.

And purple for the royal dress you now wear at the party in My house.

My paper is covered in a newfound Jesus.

There is no blue—He isn't sad.

Grays and dark shadows have disappeared.

Raise your hand if you want a new coloring page. Ask Him for a fresh start. Here is your new box of crayons and a crisp, white sheet of paper. Go on, ask Him. "What color are You?" Now...wait for it...

14

The Blood Worked

*If that first covenant had been
faultless, there would have been no
occasion to look for a second.*

HEBREWS 8:7 ESV

When Maggie was about five years old and John was nearly two, we lived in the little white house with red shutters. The backyard had huge pecan trees, and Justin kept an enormous vegetable garden. The entire yard was shadily canopied by trees that in West Texas are usually few and far between. The two children safely played on the swing set and in the sandbox while I cared for wee baby Luke. I could see them from the kitchen window where I did dishes and cooked, and also from the large family room windows when I nursed Luke while they played.

One gorgeous spring day I put Luke down for a nap while Maggie and John played outside. I had started preparing dinner when I heard John scream. I rushed outside and found him facedown and bleeding. Maggie was on the swing, pumping her little legs as fast as she could and repeatedly beating John to a pulp with the swing and her purple Nike adorned feet.

I yelled, "Mary Margaret, *stop!*"

And she smugly replied, "Park rules: Get in the way, it will ruin your day!"

My urgency to save John's life was muddled with the terror I envisioned Maggie would be as a high school sophomore. Poor John-John, unaware of the park rules, now had two black eyes and a busted lip. And Maggie had a busted bum and was in her room for the duration of the day.

We know the rules.

We are all about the rules.

When Jesus becomes Lord of your heart, and you fully grasp what happened on that cross, He won't lead you in front of the swing to be smacked in the face. He came to fulfill the law and give us life abundant. Under the old covenant, I dotted my *i*'s and crossed my *t*'s and prayed that John wouldn't get hit by a bus, promising that if he was spared I would be "good." Under the new covenant, I am righteous. The work is completed. I am obedient to callings on my life not out of terror but out of the love that seeps from me, fearlessly, because God is so good.

But...

The Holy Spirit came so we could be in constant contact with ultimate love. So why do we still wait for leaders whom we feel are somehow special or more "anointed" than we are to teach us how to approach God?

I am no closer to Jesus than anyone picking up these pages. He is no less available to you than He is to me. You don't need anyone to tell you what He's saying—His words are ready and waiting for you.

So often we let ourselves become wholly dependent on the

authority and teaching of a pastor, church leader, or even a bestselling author. Ignoring our inheritance, we believe that another person is closer to Jesus than we lowly folks could ever be.

But back before the printing press, before any seminaries, before
any Christian authority could bear that name, Jesus sent His Spirit.
He promised, "The Advocate, the Holy Spirit, whom the Father will
send in my name, will teach you all things and will remind you of
everything I have said to you" (John 14:26). Yes, seeking wise counsel is good, but Jesus is all yours already. You are absolutely equipped
to commune with Him.

> His divine power has given us everything we need for a
> godly life through our knowledge of him who called us
> by his own glory and goodness (2 Peter 1:3).

If there is anyone who is leading you to believe that you must
do one thing or another to earn favor with Jesus, that person is not
teaching the Good News.

Pastor Andrew Farley, author of *The Naked Gospel*, explained it
like this:

> There is one question I feel is imperative in understand-
> ing and building a relationship with Jesus Christ: What
> do you believe you must do to receive salvation? If you
> answer anything other than *believe*, it might be time to
> rethink the message you are hearing.[1]

Time after time, when I have been trapped in the works-based
mind-set of trying to convince myself that I could make the sacrifice of the cross more than it already is, I have found myself set free
by the truth of the Bible. The truth is in there. Test every question
against the Word. Freedom waits for you.

Christ died for us while we were still sinners.

And the blood worked.

Still, we try. We try to save ourselves, fully believing God is keeping a tally of our good works and nasty deeds. But in all His goodness, Jesus is not more or less pleased with me when I am rocking a foster baby than when I am tearing open a third bag of Cheetos. How good is this God? He knew I couldn't, so He did. And then He invited me to a banquet to indulge in His goodness. He wants to be with me. Just as I am.

Moment by moment, from one pant size to the next, the blood works. The dance is ongoing. He never leaves me or forsakes me.

> You have an anointing from the Holy One, and all of you
> know the truth (1 John 2:20).

You are the anointed.

You.

The only thing missing is the believing.

You and I are missing the opportunity to bask in freedom and run and not grow weary! Jesus counted us blameless and redeemed when we first believed. We will see Him in heaven because of this belief, and we may also see that we often missed the opportunity to fully take on the majestic wardrobe of the redeemed. If Jesus were coming to dinner, what would you wear? Your best?

Yet He is your best. Put Him fully on. Fully claim, "I am washed clean by the blood of the Lamb."

We get dunked in the cool tub behind the pulpit, and then we rush to the lobby to sign up for the next Bible study on how to overcome our sin! While we are still soaked in the living water that set us free! The water that washed us clean and counted us righteous drips onto the application for the study we will go to every Wednesday to accomplish that which was completed in the baptismal tank just moments ago. We tell people the Good News, and then we take it right back by telling them, "Now all you have to do is..."

Wait. What?

Jesus plus nothing.

The work of the cross makes the legitimate answer to every religious argument, "Just Jesus." And yet we are still deep in the trenches, working to overcome, up to our necks in what we must do. If we climb out of that bondage and continually look to what Jesus did, we are no longer part of the equation. And this is excellent news, because remember, we live in a world of sin. Our flesh still desires sin. But with His Spirit in us, we want what He wants.

We are still tormented by the very thing Jesus demolished on Calvary: sin. We have died to sin (Romans 6:2-7). We listen to the story of the Israelites and snicker, "Those foolish Israelites...they just wanted a king. Wandering in the desert, they were so blind to the fact that God was right there all along as their King." But we still beg for the same thing. We are still building golden calves and unwilling to just receive that which has been bought and paid for.

A gift.

We praise God for the gift of new life when we hold our new baby. We readily accept the mystery of a new soul, the goodness of innocence, the never-been-walked-on newborn feet, but we refuse to accept that He feels this same love for us. To God, we are the innocent because when we say yes to Jesus, we are newborn children delivered from sin and cleansed by the blood. But surely it isn't that simple.

God said I was washed in the water and cleansed by the Lamb, *but* He wants me to strive for perfection? That doesn't add up, does it? Why earn what has already been given to you through Jesus's sacrifice? If you have believed and received, then you are forgiven and set free—declared perfect because of what Christ has done for you, His beloved. If you are saved, then you are saved. If you are cleansed, then you are cleansed, period. Not Jesus, plus this and this and this.

And so many of us are quick to judge "those Catholics and their rosaries," but if you think any of part of redemption is up to your good deeds, why the cross, friend? Our Father in heaven gave more than six hundred laws, and it was too heavy. So He cut the number down to ten, and still it was too much. So instead of burying you under the work of law, He chose to set you free to commune with Him, to be counted His friend through the death of His beloved Son.

The blood worked.

Grace is the consequence.

Eternity is the prize.

I wish I weren't just imagining you were here with me. I wish you were with me right now to jump up and down and shout and weep and laugh and cry with you! Jesus knew you couldn't do it, so He did it. Now all He sees is you—clean, saved, and totally redeemed.

We are sitting on the edge of the well listening to His teaching. He has already given us the water. We are holding the chalice, yet we do not drink. We are so accustomed to the law we are begging the Holy Spirit to come—even though He is already upon us. I invited Christ into my heart in Victoria, Texas, and He stayed. Then, believing I must work to keep Him present, I morphed Him into something He wasn't and worshipped the false god that is my folly—folly that Jesus died for so that I might walk in freedom.

I was begging God to do what had already been done. I hadn't believed what I was saying. I hadn't taken off my funeral clothes and embraced the epic proportion of my birthright. The language that came out of my mouth oozed fear and doubt instead of praise and freedom.

Days before I wrote this chapter, my friend, Tracy Levinson, author of the book *Unashamed*, called me and said, "I want to pray for you." Without warning or thought, I confessed my eating struggle to her. "I have struggled with an eating disorder since I was twelve." And she said, "Ask Him to show you *what now* instead of *what then*."

If/then Jesus no more.

I am free.

In my bondage I was trying to behave so that He would bless me. In my freedom I could hear more clearly solutions that were not contingent on me but generous offers He was making to help me. Truly I confess, *I thought I had to overcome before I could seek wise counsel*. As if there was shame in seeking help in my brokenness. The sneaky snake held me captive to the work. When I believed, "Jesus, this is my struggle, which You came to conquer, it is beyond me. Show me what to do now," He did. I'd been missing out on the banquet while I was trying to overcome the slop. I kept begging for healing, but Jesus had already come and healed me. I just hadn't actually believed Him. I had talked the talk. I had cleverly insinuated that He was the Lord of my heart, and I had killed myself to keep Him there. I had lamented my heartbreak; I was incapable of overcoming something He overcame.

I knew the rules, yet I stood in front of the swing and got kicked in the face over and over.

Maybe I should have just moved away from the swings.

> Christ has set us free to live a free life. So take your stand! Never again let anyone put a harness of slavery on you.
>
> I am emphatic about this. The moment any one of you submits to circumcision or any other rule-keeping system, at that same moment Christ's hard-won gift of

freedom is squandered. I repeat my warning: The person who accepts the ways of circumcision trades all the advantages of the free life in Christ for the obligations of the slave life of the law.

I suspect you would never intend this, but this is what happens. When you attempt to live by your own religious plans and projects, you are cut off from Christ, you fall out of grace. Meanwhile we expectantly wait for a satisfying relationship with the Spirit. For in Christ, neither our most conscientious religion nor disregard of religion amounts to anything. What matters is something far more interior: faith expressed in love (Galatians 5:1-6 msg).

I am a sinner in a fallen world. Yes, I want to be different—righteous. But righteousness is not purchased by me, the sinner, by working for points or working off demerits. Salvation isn't a roadside prison crew picking up trash. It is completed through Him in me. And the essence of this is simply to believe what Christ says about me.

One of my favorite illustrations of this is the Prostitute to Princess analogy.

> Imagine that a king made a decree in his land that there would be a blanket pardon extended to all prostitutes. Would that be good news to you if you were a prostitute? Of course it would. No longer would you have to live in hiding, fearing the sheriff. No longer would you have a criminal record; all past offenses are wiped off the

books. So the pardon would definitely be good news. But would it be any motivation at all for you to change your lifestyle? No, not a bit.

But let's go a little further with our illustration. Let's say that not only is a blanket pardon extended to all who have practiced prostitution, but the king has asked you, in particular, to become his bride. What happens when a prostitute marries a king? She becomes a queen. *Now* would you have a reason for a change of lifestyle? Absolutely. It doesn't take a genius to realize that the lifestyle of the queen is several levels superior to that of a prostitute. No woman in her right mind would go back to the previous life. [2]

Does a queen sell her body to strangers?

Does royalty barter for pedigree?

Hear this: Are you changed because you have embraced the tiara? Or are you still trying to unhinge your tiara from a Target basket in ninety-mile-an-hour winds?

The fact is, you can embrace your shame under the old covenant. Or you can just believe.

We are made saints by our salvation; we just haven't renewed our minds to believe. I might carry the physical scars or battle wounds of sin, but I have been made whole by the blood of Jesus. If I believe, it is done.

On the cusp of finally embracing the reality I did not have to keep earning God's favor, one evening I shut off my alarm clock. An alarm that had been set for 5:00 a.m. so I could have quiet time with my Bible so that the deed would be counted among my works. When I woke at 7:15 instead, I bathed in contempt, disgusted with my failure. Then I ate too many pancakes, didn't shower, and curled up on the couch all day hating myself and yelling at my kids.

That night I got an e-mail from a friend. She said, "I saw this and thought I should send it to you." She included a Bible verse—Matthew 11:28.

"Come to me, all you who are weary and burdened, and I will give you rest."

I was tired.

I have a lot of kids.

My life is hectic.

Jesus was available to me all day long; He didn't mandate my rising at 5:00 a.m. to be saved.

He never leaves me.

There's not a tragedy He doesn't see.

Nothing ever lost that can't be found.

Nothing worn beyond repair.

Ground zero, He did it, I live it.

I had been given the gift of rest and counted it among my failures in my Christian walk. The suggestion that I get up at 5:00 a.m. to be alone with Jesus is not a commandment. If I wake at 5:00 and curl up with coffee and my Bible—woohoo *for me*; that's right. This is for me. I am fed by Him. But the sacrifice of the cross is done. There is nothing I can do to make it better or more brilliant. The ransom on the cross is the perfection. I can't make it more perfect.

Jesus sees me as redeemed. When I plead with Him to fix me, He says, *Of what?*

I was washed in the water, a new creation in Christ, perfected by the blood of the Lamb, and the lie I believed was that *now* the hard work had to begin. But the hard work Jesus did can't be topped.

Slashed to pieces, under the weight of His own cross, nailed to it, naked with His mother watching.

It is done.

Friend, I am no longer praying in fear; I have started praying in faith. Stop praying like a beggar and pray like the daughter of the King; a King who has already bought and paid for your royal inheritance. He told you it was done, yet you pray like the work is in your hands, and you are not worthy. But you were made righteous by the blood of the Lamb. Yes. You are awful. Yes. I am the worst. Which is the very reason why He came: to save us from ourselves. It's already done. The blessing is acknowledging my imperfections, and I rebuke the lie that I might be perfected by better understanding. But by abolishing the law, the truth is that there is nothing left for me to do but be loved and love.

There is nothing left for me to do but bask in His glory. Only then, only when I claim my birthright as *His*, do I thrive in my "wants" to be better. It is then my nature to follow Him, not because of who I am, but because of Him who dwells in me. And His goodness oozes from all of us who have accepted the gift of Jesus's sacrifice. We are convicted of, not condemned by, our sins. We are boiling over with *His* goodness, not the offense of self-righteousness. And from Him no offense comes. We aren't offensive, and we aren't offended. We peacefully walk in the light of our inheritance, and we fear not! We grieve with the *hope* of Him drawing us near. Nothing can knock the wind from our lungs. Why? Because He continually breathes new life into us!

Manacled to a pew with my latte in hand, I used to shout hallelujah at a teaching that died with Him on the cross. But the Spirit did not come to help us cope with the law. The Spirit came to give freedom from the law that we might walk in the abundance of peace in Jesus Christ.

Stop the great terror and step into the Light.

It's All Grace

Grace is a lovely contradiction of brilliance and folly. Sometimes grace is forgiveness. The way a parent forgives a child—or a God forgives humanity. Other times grace is an apology, even when it was not deserved. Sometimes it is discipline, more than you were warranted or much less than you can fathom. Sometimes it is poetic, descriptive, and fascinating. Other times it appears to have completely missed the gravity of the situation.

One time grace is innocent and blind.

The next time it is passionate and expressive—definite in its beliefs.

Moreover, grace seems to go on and on, boundlessly blazing, missing opportunities to veer off and come to a stop, traveling far beyond the reasonable. If I were to have only met grace once, I might think it one way or another. I may have believed it merely forgiveness or a blanket statement for escaping punishment. Then I met with it again, and it was something else.

Most recently, I sat alone, merely as a spectator, at a meeting for the broken, the weary, the addicted. From the outside, it is easy to judge. From the inside, I know I am no different. I am in need of grace in all of its complexities. I am desperate for every definition and every exploration by which it is exposed.

To define grace in essay or in word is to assume you can fathom how cavernous and profound it expands.

Grace is yours. You are the anointed. Again I say to you: It is yours. You don't need anyone to tell you He is calling or what He is saying—He picked you. He offers you the most frivolous and beautifully confusing gift—grace.

Imagine if every time you sat down to visit with your child, you talked at length about what you expected from him and how awful he'd behaved, and all the things he needed to do differently in order for you to spend time with him. What would that relationship look like? Furthermore, what if he had a list of ways you had to behave in order to continue the relationship?

The Vandals, Sam and Charlie, love to bring me gifts. While playing outside they collect tiny wildflowers and, well, weeds and bring them to me. They giggle with delight when I stick them in my hair or tuck a dandelion behind my ear. To bestow these gifts on me is the epitome of blessing to these young boys. Five minutes before they bless me with the tiny bits of nature they have plucked, I could have been a raging lunatic over the state of their room. Still they only want to give me good things!

Likewise, my older children like to bring me coffee, help with dishes after dinner, or surprise Justin and me with the offer to watch the younger children while we go to dinner. And you know the old saying, "It is better to give than to receive." How much do you love to love on those you love? Stop for a moment and ponder the greatest surprise you were ever able to give someone you cared about. Don't dwell on their human reaction; think about the feelings you had when you were in the position of giving!

Imagine if you sat before a human you love more than anyone else in the world and handed them a bag full of one million dollars cash. You haven't slept because of the vibration of anticipation. You are consumed with the notion you are about to give something that is going to change this person's life—forever. You want nothing more than to pour out this grand expression of generosity. You sit down and hand them the bag. They thank you, but they don't open the bag. Instead, they push it aside and begin to lament their financial woes to you. They cry about how desperate they are for money. Then they go on to list every single financial mistake they have ever made.

This is what we do every time we decide to ignore the gift of grace. We push the bag full of abundance aside.

Grace upon Grace

Make no mistake: Those who have believed are indeed saved. But like the other brother, Lloyd, we wander the halls of our Father's house playing the martyred role of slave instead of a son—we never dine in the banquet hall. Instead, we feast on the sorrows of self at the pity party or acclaim our praise at the soul-sucking piety party, and we are never satisfied. Our cup is half empty and never overflows.

All we have is His, not because of what we do, but because of what He did. By His stripes, our sins were forgotten and are *continually* forgiven. We cannot do anything else but take off our funeral clothes and put on our party garb. Only then does the chalice overflow. We cannot be made any more perfect than the spotless Lamb who was sacrificed on behalf of our rancid sin. No good deed, no fast, no vigil—nothing can improve us. It is done.

And all should be well. We should be made whole by the belief we are enough where we are. How we are may be refined and sanctified as He moves, not as we move. In my fear, in my shortcomings, I believed. I believed in a virgin birth, the miracles, the signs and wonders, and the torture, death, and resurrection of Jesus Christ. That belief bought my salvation. Still, I did not fully believe in the gift of His utmost *grace*.

Grace doesn't offend. It is not religious or led by law or governed by man. Grace is precious and dear. The piety partygoers are confused by the abundance. They won't want to hear this message. They have worked too hard to overcome and strived to look like all was well when it wasn't.

If you are walking boldly in the message of grace, if you are in step with what God has for your life, why fall prey to the lie you must "do this" to fix yourself? In my soul I finally came to the place where I knew I was free. I was crazy in love with the best Jesus, Real Jesus.

Now I hear only this: *Join in the dance, My love, grace upon grace.*

So you have total license to wander aimlessly about eating éclairs and ordering clothes on a near maxed-out credit card, lusting after Dr. McDreamy on *Grey's Anatomy* and blissfully ignoring His call?

Yes.

No! (Just wanted to make sure you were still paying attention.)

Conviction and condemnation are not the same thing. There is no condemnation in Christ Jesus. When I asked Him to save me, He did.

Again and again, I say to you: *It is done; He did it.*

He will do it.

The rest is grace upon grace.

15

Sweet Jesus

*Blessed are those who mourn, for
they will be comforted.*

Matthew 5:4

I'd be lying if I said I liked to hurt, but I do love to be close to Jesus. And the simple reality is that I am nearer to Him in my suffering.

When I first met Justin, his mom confided in me that he was coming off of a horrible breakup. According to her, Justin had gone to a strip club with his college roommates and met a stripper named Candy. Candy was a single mother of a three-year-old girl named Lucy. So, in love with Candy and Lucy, and desperate to save Candy from the strip club nightlife, Justin was working an extra night job to support the wayward duo. He bought them groceries and had encouraged Candy to get her cosmetology license; he even paid for her first semester of beauty school. One night after Justin had been to class all day and then worked two jobs, he came home to find a note from Candy. She thanked him for his preciousness and wished him well. She apologized for wasting his money on tuition, but she and Lucy were moving to San Antonio with her ex-boyfriend. She could make much more money there at a "gentlemen's club."

If I was crazy about Justin before, my adoration quadrupled. But in light of this disclosure from his mother, I decided then and there he needed space to grieve. I broke a date with him, told him that I wasn't ready to date seriously, and went to a party with Lisa, Justin's cousin, my roommate. I was sad. But I didn't want to be Justin's rebound gal.

When Lisa and I got back to our apartment at two in the morning, Justin was sitting on the stairwell. He looked so heartbroken. Lisa excused herself and went inside, and I sat down next to the sweetest guy on the planet. He asked flatly, "Did I do something wrong? I thought we were having a really good time."

Poor guy.

"Justin," I said, my voice cracking, "you are so wonderful. But I think that you are not grieving properly. I like you so much, but I think it's best that you spend some time alone. Losing Candy and Lucy isn't something you get over in just a few months. And I don't want to be a rebound." He started to speak, and I dramatically raised my fingers to his lips and shushed him. "Let's talk next semester," I whispered.

Biting back tears, I theatrically stood to go into my apartment when I heard him say, "Who are Candy and Lucy?"

Yup.

Justin's older brother, Josh, made the whole story up in an elaborate prank on their mom.

This was one of Josh's favorite stories. He thought it was hilarious.

Josh was killed in a car accident in 2009. His death was a horrific trial for our family. At his funeral, we went around and told tales of him, some taller than others. Finally it was my turn, and I wanted to tell the Candy and Lucy story.

But I couldn't. It was a story that always brought everyone to belly laughs, but suddenly it was a story I wanted all to myself.

We all have our own ways of grieving.

Recently, at a funeral for a friend's husband who died too young and unexpectedly, one of the funeral goers asked her, "What are you going to do now?"

Our mind-set dictates that we need a plan. We need a method to get out of the madness and back onto the life of abundance. To answer the question, "What are you going to do now?" with the simple statement, "Grieve" is not acceptable in our culture. In our society, we are pressured to move on to the next thing. The American dream doesn't include "hurting." Many seem to associate grief with a pity party. *Just get over it—and fast!*

Another friend of mine who buried her little boy was given seventy-two hours off of work for bereavement. Her boss sent flowers with a note that said, "We look forward to your return and for things to get back to normal for you."

My friend, counselor and author Paul Mathis, recently wrote:

> My dad, who is wiser than I will ever be, told me after my brother's funeral that he just accepted everything everyone said to him because he knew their intent. He did not agree with everything he heard, but he knew the people speaking to him were trying to find something nice to say. So I have been able to practice that for me. But I certainly do hope I can encourage others to never say the things that were said to us. I have decided that if I am ever going to quote a scripture at somebody in a time of grief, it will be "Jesus wept." Because that's all anyone at a funeral needs to know.[1]

Don't let them see you cry.
Dry your eyes.

It'll be okay.

All things work together for good.

She is in a better place.

Granted, most people don't know what to say, and so they come across as misguided. But perhaps that is the issue. That we feel we must say, and we must do, and we need to pick up and trudge on, apply new mascara and at least act like we have it all together. I would like to suggest that as you delve into the project of meeting Jesus, be prepared to do it at the foot of the cross. And bring Kleenex.

Jesus is there. He promises us that we are blessed when we mourn. Not allowing ourselves time to grieve and have foul, gut-wrenching cries might make the people around us more comfortable, but we are missing out on Real Jesus interactions where He alone can heal us and hold us up.

Several years ago a woman in our church lost her adult son to cancer. I went to a prayer vigil and found her laid out on the floor, wailing. I didn't know what to do. My instinct was to go to her, to try to comfort her. But instead, I knelt down to pray. Her bellows echoed off every wall in that empty chapel, and I worried, if she ever finished, would she be humiliated that I had been there to witness the scene?

Bless her, she heaved sobs until she couldn't cry another tear. I sat in silence. When she sat up and crawled to the pew, we made eye contact, and I smiled softly. She smiled back and said, "Mama tears." If it had been me, I would have apologized for the scene. But she wasn't sorry, nor should she have been. She'd rested at the foot of the cross and grieved like it would kill her...and she didn't die.

Blessed are those who mourn, for they will be comforted.

Jesus wept too. He grieved at the death of His friend Lazarus. And I don't understand that part of the story at all, because right after He wept, He went to Lazarus's grave and raised him from the dead.

Why did He weep? Why was He sad? He knew what was going to happen next, didn't He?

He cried because He loved. His goodness wasn't the cause of Lazarus's death. He wept because He grieved death and He lamented mourning.

I'm glad He wept. I am glad that He is of such grand character that He muddled through His emotions and that He grieved. I think about this aspect of Him often. When I hear of such great suffering, I take comfort that I worship a God who experienced human grief to the point of tears.

And grief doesn't come only at the funeral. I weep at full gravesites, yes, but also at empty cradles. Currently, we are losing a long-term foster placement. We love this little girl. She loves us. And when I think about losing her I get sad. *Really sad.* I bawl like no one is watching and pour out my heart to a God who loves her a billion times more than I do. He can see the snapshots in my mind—the first time I laid eyes on her, the first time she reached for me, her resting in my arms. No one else can see these pictures, but God knows this little girl even better than I know her. And He listens to my pleas to take care of her, to go with her, and to manifest the seed we planted in her heart to know Him. When she is gone, I will want and need to grieve her. I will be sad not to be with her when she loses her first tooth, learns to ride a bike, or meets the love of her life. I need to grieve that loss.

And that baby's cradle won't be the only empty bed in my home. My oldest, Maggie, recently moved to Oxford for school, living an ocean away. People kept telling me how much fun she'd have and reassuring me that we can still FaceTime. Yes, thumbs-up for technology. Now, if that technology would only make her footsteps echo in my hall, place her head on the pillow in her childhood bedroom, or rewind history so I could play with her in the backyard or review her Latin vocabulary one more time.

I am sad. I miss her. Her travels ended a season in my life, a season I adored. Of course, I raised her to go. Of course, I want her to have an adventure and learn and grow, but that doesn't negate my feelings of loss.

Grief is our least favorite practice.

It is no fun.

It is mysterious.

It isn't ideal or tidy, but it is necessary.

On the day my brother-in-law Josh died, I escaped to the front porch. The house was brimming with shock and grief, and I had to get someplace quiet. I saw one of my best friends, Marcy, driving up the long ranch drive, and I ran to her. As I heaved my heartache, I asked her, "What will become of my children? So many bad things keep happening. How can I protect them?"

Marcy, in her wisdom and love of truth in the Word, pulled away, looked me straight in my swollen eyes, and knew exactly what my problem was. It wasn't that I wanted to protect them from car accidents—no, it was that I didn't trust God to keep them safe. Marcy knew who I wanted to protect my children from. So she said, "Stop believing in a wrathful God!"

When did I first believe He was anything but good? In this life I will face trials and tribulation, but He never said He was going to cause it. No, He said, "This stuff will happen, sweet girl, but I have overcome the world" (John 16:33, my paraphrase).

I built a case against my Father in heaven based on flippant things people said at funerals, misquoted scriptures, and bad theology. Now I sit in my prayer chair and stare at Stolen Jesus with a new confidence. The world is a mess, children get cancer, orphans wander in the wilderness, young girls are sold as sex slaves, and still He loved the world so much He sent His only Son to die and overcome those awful things and provide hope and restoration.

I still wonder why those bad things happen. But He moves how He moves and He saves how He saves. I need only believe in the sovereignty of God and His favor. I vow to speak truth and blessing over my life and the lives of my children. I cease to believe that He is a Father that breaks legs or dishes out brain tumors in an effort to teach a grand lesson.

In the midst of my suffering, suffering He didn't manifest, He comes only to comfort. Should tragedy strike, sweet Jesus will be comfort. He is enough. He is all.

I remember everything about the day.

My babies stood in a line dressed in funeral clothes. They fidgeted in front of the coffin. They behaved like, well, children at a funeral—out of place. The boys tugged at their ties. At one point I noticed that Luke had fastened his clip-on to the crotch of his pants, causing his brother to snort-laugh. I snapped my fingers and shot him a glare, knowing full well their Uncle Josh, the guest of honor at this funeral, would have more than approved.

Come to think of it, my brother-in-law probably told Luke to wear clip-ons for this very reason.

When the service ended, I straightened myself and the children so people could shuffle past us with their condolences.

"What a lovely service."

Yes, thank you.

"Josh would have loved all these flowers."

Yes, he would have, thank you.

"All things work together for good, you know."

My heart pounded. My eyes burned. Bile rose in my throat. I didn't know that scripture could cut me. I was barely able to function from the weight of this catastrophe, and I was supposed to rejoice in God's good plan?

I hated that verse. And I was overcome with guilt for thinking so.

In my grief, in my disappointment, in my hopelessness, I don't want to hear that He will make it for my good. But still, in His sovereignty, I have to trust that He *can*. So maybe this is the most honest prayer I can pray: "I don't believe it. So show me how it is true. Teach me things I have not known. Forgive my trespasses. And help me not to ever break someone's heart or lead them further from You. Let me never steal Jesus from someone who needs Him."

The world's tragedies are where God shows Himself strong. This is where He cares for me with kid gloves and abundant mercy. If the worst-case scenario is death, I need only remember two things:

He conquered death.

And He came to bind up my broken heart.

⎯⎯⎯

Maggie has this extremely unusual superpower. Nothing stings her. One evening several years ago we were watching a movie, and she kept getting up, adjusting her sweatshirt, and then sitting back down to continue watching. After about the seventh time, my husband inquired, "Mags, what are you doing?"

And Maggie replied, "I feel this weird sensation. Like someone is lightly popping me with a rubber band." We ignored her. Still, she persisted. Finally, unable to concentrate on the movie with her twitching, Justin flipped on the light. To our horror, she had a huge scorpion on her!

I rushed into the bathroom with her to see how badly she'd been stung. With no less than twenty-two little red pin marks, Maggie was okay. She wasn't hurt, swelling, itching, or showing adverse allergic responses. Me? This would have resulted in a trip to the hospital. If I get bitten by an ant, I go into asthmatic trauma. I made her bathe and gave her precautionary Benadryl. After she was dressed in clean pajamas, she came back in to finish the movie.

For those who have ever been stung by a scorpion, this is shocking. It hurts. *Badly.* For me, on the one occasion I was stung in high school, the injury could have had a deadly result. Before a megadose of antihistamine, my tongue began to swell, my face and neck got purple, and my voice became raspy. I am not sure why, but after I have had an allergic emergency, the bottoms of my feet hurt so badly I am unable to walk for at least twenty-four hours. I'd say that a scorpion sting is kind of like a rubber-band pop, but less, "Well, that is an irritating sensation" and more like, "THAT HURTS LIKE NOTHING I HAVE EVER EXPERIENCED! MAKE IT STOP!"

Three days later Maggie was stung by a wasp. We were in the pool, and she accidentally put her hand on it. She yelped. But then nothing.

A week or so later Luke was stung by a wasp, and his hand was so swollen he couldn't bend his fingers or pick anything up. It took three doses of Benadryl before the swelling finally subsided. More recently my dad was hunting and was stung by some bees. He felt like he was dying and for two days he could barely stay awake. He was nauseated, itchy, and exhausted.

Ants, bees, wasps, and scorpions' stings have no effect on Maggie.

Now it is like a party trick at our house. If the mosquitoes are out, guests can watch as she allows one to suck the nectar that is her sweet blood and never get a bump or itch. We usually only pull this rabbit out of the hat when the cable is out and it's too late to start a game of Monopoly. We're kind of curious if she would fare just as well if she were bitten by a rattlesnake. (I propose we not find out.) It's a unique trait.

The apostle Paul, writing to the Corinthians, cried,

> "Where, O death, is your victory?
> Where, O death, is your sting?"
>
> The sting of death is sin, and the power of sin is the law.
> But thanks be to God! He gives us the victory through
> our Lord Jesus Christ (1 Corinthians 15:55-57).

The scorpion isn't going anywhere—not yet at least. But his stings can't touch us.

In the past, when we have had money trouble or walked through a difficult season, I could watch the scale creep up because my help came from cookies. Even today I might need Xanax to get on a plane. I fear many things, but I do not fear grief like I did before. Perhaps it is because the grief of the past is something I see differently now. Before, when I was hurt, I believed one of the Jesus personas was punishing me. This lie held me captive. Now I am confident my help comes from Him. I don't want cookies. (Well, I still want cookies, but not to mask the opportunity to be comforted by Jesus.) I want Jesus.

In the midst of my grief, He heals.

Let me testify to that healing with this fact: I just mailed a letter to John, my now nineteen-year-old son—the same son I feared would never see his tenth birthday. The letter contained encouragement,

Scripture, and my belief that he is trudging through a season of grand design. The calling he is currently pursuing is one I wish he could have been spared. But my letter to him was written in total confidence—confidence in his well-being, abilities, and eternal home. I couldn't manifest this confidence and faith by myself when this boy was safely tucked in his bed wearing footed Spider-Man pajamas. But now, with Real Jesus, I have absolute assurance in his well-being—even though this letter is headed to him at Marine boot camp. His goal? Humanitarian aid. And when he received his desired assignment, Combat Engineer, I squealed...with delight.

I am free of my fears because He is real.

So go and have an ugly, snot-flinging, heaving cry. Cry until you barf. Blow your nose on your sheets. Get in bed and wail and let Jesus be Jesus and pour out grace upon grace upon grace to you, His baby. Don't apologize. Don't be sorry. Just be sad. He will restore you. He will rebuild that which was taken, and He will provide comfort and healing in an ordained time and in ways you cannot fathom. Sorrow will be turned into dancing and joy will come in the morning.

The only challenge before you?

Believe.

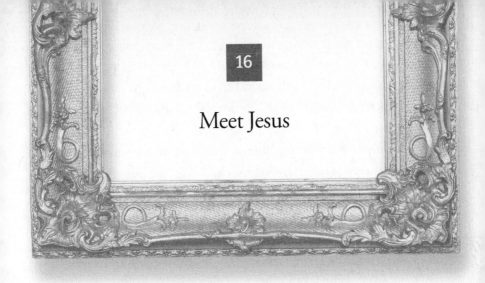

16

Meet Jesus

Now we see in a mirror dimly, but then face
to face. Now I know in part; then I shall
know fully, even as I have been fully known.

1 CORINTHIANS 13:12 ESV

My youngest son, Charlie, is all mamma's boy. Vandal that he is, his is also such a sweet and tender spirit. He is a cuddle bug and truly loves to be in my arms, playing with my hair and caressing my cheeks. He will say through puckered lips, "Gimme a widdle kiss, Mommy." He continues to melt my heart.

He is stunningly beautiful, and like his birth father, incredibly intelligent. We are confident he will be our easiest to school. Daily Charlie shocks us with his high-level thinking and problem-solving abilities.

His voice is another of his comedic, adorable, and endearing traits. It's raspy and scratchy. Charlie sounds like he smokes a pack a day. He loves coffee, and he will wander to my room every morning to say, "Mom, I need some caupee. Mom, you hear me? I gots to have some caupee." My husband and I can barely contain the giggles. We keep waiting to find him on the back porch watching the sun rise with a cup of "caupee," reading *USA Today*.

The only thing that continues to baffle us is how sorry he is. I have never seen a more apologetic child. Charlie puts himself in time-out on a pretty regular basis. I can stroll through the kitchen at any given moment and find him with his nose in the corner. We call it the self-inflicted time-out. When this happens, it is essential that we go locate the baby. If Charlie is in time-out, the baby probably has been painted hot pink, duct-taped to the ceiling, colored blue and green with permanent markers, or had her head shaved. Hence the aforementioned nickname of "The Vandals."

I dropped a glass the other day, and Charlie said, "Oh! Sworry bout dat, Mommy!" Another time the older Vandal, Sam, and he got in a fight over a fire truck, and Sam clawed Charlie's arm to the point of drawing blood. I punished Sam while Charlie cried in the background, "Swoorry, Mommy. Sworry, Sam. I sworry 'bout dat!"

More recently, I was out of town for a few days, and when he saw me pull in the driveway he started screaming, "Mommy is home! Mommy is home!" As he raced toward me, he tripped over the garden hose, skinning his knees and hands and leaving an enormous goose egg on his forehead. I scooped him up to love on him, and he repeatedly cried, "I sworry, Mommy, I so sworry." I couldn't make him understand he'd done nothing wrong. In my eyes, he was utterly blameless. I didn't want his apologies; I wanted to comfort him. Sure, he needed to learn to watch where he was going. But I wasn't condemning him! He was terribly hurt and needed only to let me love on him and dress his wounds. Still, he wouldn't quit apologizing. His raspy voice pled with me to forgive his stumbling, and it tore at my heart. I love my son, and I don't want him to keep apologizing for things that aren't any of his doing.

Which brings me to confession.

Confession continues to carry much baggage for me. And while I no longer submit to the idea that I need to go to a priest, I am often convicted of my need to recall my sins repeatedly. Just like Charlie's continual apologies leave me feeling as though I haven't shown him enough love, I consider this when I approach confession with the counterfeit Jesuses of my past.

Imagine if every single time I sat down with one of my children the conversation went like this:

> ME: Tell me everything you've ever done wrong.
>
> CHILD: I stole gum, I cheated on my spelling test, and I talked about the neighbor behind her back.
>
> ME: Tell me you are sorry.
>
> CHILD: I am so sorry.
>
> ME: Tell me it won't ever happen again.
>
> CHILD: It won't ever happen again.
>
> ME: Tell me what you need.
>
> CHILD: Gas money, tuition, and some socks.
>
> ME: Have you done anything good?
>
> CHILD: I mowed the lawn.
>
> ME: Yes, but you gossiped about the neighbor. I'll think about it. I may or may not bless you, or...I may sprain your ankle so you won't forget how I feel about your sin.

Ugh.

I wouldn't see that child much. Why? Because that isn't a relationship. That is a dictatorship.

Confess, in the original Hebrew, is the word *yadah*. It can also be translated as *praise, give thanks, glorify,* or *be in agreement.* Casts a different light on the whole task, doesn't it? Confession shouldn't be muttering my sins under my breath. No—with a freed heart and fresh eyes, my confession should be a hymn of thanksgiving, praising and glorifying the Father with open hands, in agreement.

In confession, I agree with Jesus that I need Him. I praise Him that while I still sinned, He laid down His life for mine. I agree that I am washed clean by the blood of the Lamb. I am sorry for my sins, and I give praise for the continued work that Jesus will do in me, convicting me and correcting me when I am wrong but never condemning me for that which He conquered on the cross.

The cross of my salvation.

Grace upon grace.

As has already been established, I say loony things to my kids. The other night I barked at the Vandals, "If you don't go to bed, I am going to dig my eyes out with a spoon! Someone hand me a spoon!"

And sweet Sam looked around and said, "I don't gots a spoon, Mommy, but here is a fly swapper. It will probably work." He demonstrated by jabbing his eye with the end of the tool. Well-meaning and dear, it was an option, I suppose, but not the legitimate solution to my problem. (Bed. Bed was the legitimate solution to my problem.)

In our world, in this creation, sin is the problem. All have sinned; all have fallen short. And as Romans 6:23 so chillingly promises, "The wages of sin is death."

But in Christ, God has given us the answer. Jesus is the legitimate solution to every problem. And Jesus is not some faceless idol.

He knows me, and greater still, I firmly believe He craves my knowledge of Him. The *real* Him. I walk in freedom because He craved me to His death.

So now, at last, the worst-case scenario has been faced and conquered. Death has no sting when we are certain of eternity. Sight can be restored even after we have dug our own eye out with a fly swapper because of *who He is.*

Perhaps I went the long way. I still hold Jesus in reverence, and I fear Him in a new and healthy way. Not in a condemning and wrathful way. I imagine this will be an ongoing process. Imagine the confession of the new covenant.

> Jesus: Hello, love.
>
> Me: Did You see me yelling at the kids? I am so sorry.
>
> Jesus: I know. And I forgive you. That's why I came.
>
> Me: It won't ever happen again.
>
> Jesus: Yes, it will, and when you confess, I'll forgive you all over again.
>
> Me: Jesus, did You hear? John joined the Marines. And our foster-love is leaving soon. And I sprained my ankle.
>
> Jesus: Yes, I'll go with John. I think he is a great kid. I know it is scary, but you can rest. I got this. No matter what, I have it. And, Jami, that goes for the baby too. Within the seeds you've planted is the entire plant. I am taking care of all of it, no charge. Bought and paid for. And I am so sorry about your ankle. Stay off it, ice it, give yourself a break.

No condemnation. No groveling. A relationship with the Divine who lived and died for you and me to have life abundant. Salvation. This is not a mean God. This is a God of mercy. Reject the lie: God didn't make your car break down in a ditch so He could show you something. Yes, He may use stinking situations to reveal something to us, but He is only good.

God is good.

The devil is bad.

Jesus died so that I might live as the righteous.

The devil doesn't want me to walk in this freedom.

Jesus loves me. Perfect love casts out all fear. And if He is for me...who shall be against me?

Oh, goodness! Look how I have gone on and on.

I imagine our visit is over, the chocolate is all gone, and it's too late to start another pot of coffee. And look, Real Jesus just pulled up in front of my house. He's in an old pickup. (He appreciates the reliability of American-made, you know.) We step out onto the porch and exchange hugs. The warm evening air is alive with mountain cedar and honeysuckle.

I whisper my good-bye to you. "Go in freedom, my friend, grace upon grace." The sky is bold with purple, orange, and pink, and the crickets chirp a melodious song of praise. I walk you to the drive.

Real Jesus winks from the driver's seat. I open the door, and it squeaks on aged hinges. You slide in next to Him, ready for the new covenant ride, and He flashes *that smile* and says, "Hey there, Love, buckle up! This is where it gets good."

Afterword

We recently moved back into our old house on our ranch. As I unpacked my office, I opened a box, and immediately under the packing paper I uncovered my cherished copy of *I Dare You*. And I sat on the floor and cried an ugly, snot-flinging, heaving cry. When I finished, I made a new list of Dares.

1. *Dare to be like Kim.* She didn't let the outside forces ultimately dictate who Jesus was. She went back to the beginning of the Bible. She asked questions, even if they were politically incorrect.

2. *Dare to forgive.* Check. I had already turned this one over to God.

3. *Dare to grieve.* And I mean really grieve. Let out the ugly, snot-flinging, heaving cry.

My sister, Stacey, and I recently sat down for breakfast with three of our new covenant newfound friends: Tracy Levinson and John and Bev Sheasby. John asked us what we needed to know most, and my sister said, "All of it! I want to understand this message of truth right now, all of it!" John laughed and with his gorgeous South African accent purred, "It just takes time."

Time.

And this is hard for me. I have spent all of these years trying so hard to please God, and here I am with nothing left to do. He sees me as righteous. What I do or do not do doesn't change His complete belief—I am righteous.

Days later a struggle began to brew in our home. I sat on the floor of my closet and cried and asked Jesus what to do. How do I fix this mess? Fast? Tithe? Study more Scripture? The answer came in a breath of comfort: *Believe.*

This is the essence of a change of mind. If today you learned you were a billionaire and the queen of an undiscovered kingdom with a royal court and servants, would you not behave differently? This is the difference. Instead of "trying hard" to be righteous, I accept my inheritance of righteous. This is freedom. JESUS DIED FOR ME! I am a new creation because of who He is. This is so overwhelming I cannot live in my old funeral clothes. I am a billionaire, and I behave as such. Royalty. And I am not pompous. This is because of who He is—and He dwells in me.

Weeks after our breakfast meeting, trouble was still simmering on the homefront. Justin walked in our bedroom and took one look at me and said, "Jami, why are you so happy?" By all accounts there wasn't much to be happy about. But I couldn't contain my joy. The blood worked. And because of that, it is well with me.

At every turn of my new covenant journey, I have chosen belief. Abraham was counted righteous simply because he believed. As I have encountered so many transitions in the last few months of this writing process, I am stunned at who I have become. I am not panic stricken, and I am utterly undone by the God I did not know. He is all good. And I am made whole by Him alone.

God knows where each of us are in our walk. He is not frantic that we are missing something, and He isn't worried about what will become of us. He knows it is done. And if any part of a message leaves you thinking, "Hmmmm...I don't know..." ask Him. He will show you the truth, and the truth will set you free.

So if you were to sit across from me now and ask me, "What do I do now? If I am no longer a slave to the law, do I get up and study Scripture or sleep late? Can I have pie for dinner, or do I have to eat my broccoli?" My answer is this: Ask the Real Jesus for advice on everything. From what to eat to what to wear. And then be still and let Him parent you. Believe He created you for this relationship with Him.

Believe Him.

Go on, I dare you.

May your floors be sticky and your calling ordained.

Love,
Jami

Notes

Chapter 5: High School Jesus

1. William H. Danforth, *I Dare You,* 12th Edition (St. Louis, MO; 1945), 11.

Chapter 9: Idol Jesus

1. Patricia Gunn, *Unveiling Jesus* (Grand Junction, TN: Unveiling Jesus LLC, 2014), 48.

Chapter 12: Just Jesus

1. Tracy Levinson, *Unashamed* (Denver, CO: TBL Publishing, 2016), 19.

Chapter 14: The Blood Worked

1. Andrew Farley, private interview with author.
2. Bob George, *Classic Christianity* (Eugene, OR: Harvest House Publishers, 1989), 72-73.

Chapter 15: Sweet Jesus

1. Paul Mathis, asecondtimepaul.com., private interview with author.

Acknowledgments

Special thanks to my family. Justin, I adore you, love of my life, keeper of my heart. Maggie, Christian, John, Luke, Sophie, Sam, Charlie, and our little foster-love—you are breath, story, and inspiration. I am sorry I have told all your secrets, but I really do have a fund for your counseling. Thank you, Mom and Dad, Stacey and Dean, Michael and Kelly, and the Pixies and Vandals for your prayers and support. I couldn't be more in love with each of you. To my cousin-in-law Lisa Williamson—look what you've done. Thank you, Peaches. To my friends and sisters Kim Phelan, Marcy Toppert, Lisa Carroll, Stephanie Cranfill, Bobbi Pledger, Mandy McLean, Candy Gilbert, Holly Blackwell, Teresa Donaghey, Dorothy Wilson, Cindy Miller, Daisy Blair, and Rebekah Porter—your prayers, friendship, and wisdom have made me better.

To my unruly band of wordsmith sisters, Kelly Balarie, Katie Reid, Christy Mobley, Angela Parlin, Shelby Spear , Wynema Clark, Trisha Gunn, Anna LeBaron, Angela Nazworth, Karina Allen, Abby McDonald, Fayrene Clark-Reese, Lorraine Reep, Rebecca Huff, Tracy Levinson, Shontell Brewer, Christine Carter, Jan Greenwood,

Jenny Rapsome, Christine Shuhan, and Katrina Ryder—I love you all. Katrina, you were right.

To my Facebook friends and Hopelively gang—next to Real Jesus, you are the best part of this ride.

To John and Beverly Sheasby, your words and ministry change lives. Grace upon grace, my friends.

Special thanks to John Vonhof, Kathy Ide, Judy Morrow, Xochi Dixon, Carrie Talbot, Marci Seither, Kay Marshall Strom, Kathi Lipp, Susanna Foth Aughtmon, and all the beautiful people at Mount Hermon Christian Writer's Conference.

And much gratitude and love for Jessica Kirkland, my friend and agent.

Kathleen Kerr, my friend and editor, you are the best.

And all the fabulous crew at Harvest House Publishers. You are just good people.

Most assuredly I must thank You, my God and love. Real Jesus, You are everything; so glad to have found You.

About the Author

Jami Amerine is the author of the popular blog *Sacred Ground, Sticky Floors*, where she posts about Jesus, parenting, marriage, and the general chaos of life. She holds a master's degree in education, counseling, and human development and recently began doctoral studies in Marriage and Family Counseling. Jami and her husband, Justin, have six kids and are active in foster care.

To learn more about Jami Amerine or
to read sample chapters, visit our website at
www.harvesthousepublishers.com